GROWING UP
BELOW
SEA
LEVEL

RACHEL BIALE

Growing Up
Below
Sea
Level

A KIBBUTZ CHILDHOOD

Mandel Vilar Press

The paper used in this book meets the minimum requirements of ANSI/NISO Z39.48-1992 (R1997). ∞

Cover design/illustration by Sophie Appel

Unless otherwise noted, the illustrations in this book are photographs from the author's family collections.

"The Hungarians" first appeared in *Persimmon Tree: An Online Magazine of the Arts for Women Over Sixty*, spring 2016, https://persimmontree.org/spring-2016/the-hungarians/.

Publisher's Cataloging-in-Publication Data
Names: Biale, Rachel, author.
Title: Growing up below sea level : a kibbutz childhood / Rachel Biale.
Description: Simsbury, Connecticut : Mandel Vilar Press, [2020] | Includes
    bibliographical references.
Identifiers: ISBN 9781942134633 | ISBN 9781942134640 (ebook)
Subjects: LCSH: Biale, Rachel—Childhood and youth. | Kibbutzim—History—
    20th century. | Jewish children—Israel—Biography. | Jewish refugees—
    Israel—History—20th century. | Communal living—Israel—History—20th
    century. | Israel—Social life and customs—20th century. | LCGFT:
    Autobiographies.
Classification: LCC HX742.2.K4 B53 2020 (print) | LCC HX742.2.K4 (ebook) |
    DDC 307.776092 B—dc23

Printed in the United States of America
20 21 22 23 24 25 26 27 28 / 9 8 7 6 5 4 3 2 1

Mandel Vilar Press
19 Oxford Court, Simsbury, Connecticut 06070
www.americasforconservation.org | www.mvpublishers.org

In memory of my parents,
Anina and Chaim (Kurt),
and my brother Eran

AUTHOR'S NOTE

These stories are based on recollections of my own youth. Some of the stories have been conflated with others or partially fictionalized in this narrative. One story, "Escape from the Children's House," fuses a real event (our escapade and the caretaker's extreme reaction) with unrelated, historically based accounts of the pharmacy at the Kraków Ghetto and the ghetto's liquidation in March 1943. All names, excepting those of public figures, my own, and those of my family members and of family friends Navah and Uri Haber-Schaim, as well as the kibbutz member nicknamed "Czech," were changed to protect people's privacy and confidentiality.

CONTENTS

PREFACE

The summer following third grade, our class reached the coveted status of "real workers." We were assigned to work in different branches of the kibbutz, not just in the children's farm, where we'd worked every weekday afternoon since first grade. I got one of the most prized spots: working with the dairy cows. Mostly I shadowed the grown-ups, spreading hay in the feed trough, shoveling cow patties, and washing udders with a high-pressure hose before the cows were harnessed to the milking machines. But one day something changed. Perhaps someone didn't show up for the afternoon shift, or the *raftan* (dairy worker) decided I was responsible beyond my years. Whatever it was, he told me to go out in the afternoon and bring the cows from the grazing pasture back to the milking parlor.

I walked out to the clover field, armed with a long stick and instructions on how to open and close gates in the proper order. I was assured the cows would, almost on the their own, navigate the road home.

"Moo," the cow at the front of the herd bellowed.

"*Nu!*" I yelled right back, "*Yallah,* go home!" I added a nudge, poking her behind lightly with my stick. She started trudging forward. I led the way.

Part of me can still feel my glee as I marched at the head of the herd, opening one gate, then running to the back to close the previous one after the last cow had passed it, then to the front again. Another part easily conjures up the knots in my stomach: barely over four feet high and sixty pounds, I was followed by over a hundred cows, each nearly twice my height and weighing around 1,500 pounds.

I delivered them to the cowshed safely; not one had strayed off course. Now expansive pride replaced the cramps of anxiety. Soon fatigue spread through every layer of tissue. It felt wonderful—a tiredness of great accomplishment and of "real work." In my heart I still cherish that feeling today, but my head shakes, as if of its own accord: *What were they thinking?*

The same split animates my memories of how, as very young children, we took care of each other on our own in the children's house with no adults in sight. But, as a mother and recent grandmother, I am flabbergasted. How could our parents have left us (at age four!) unsupervised from 8:00 to 10:00 every evening and from 4:00 to 6:00 every dawn? How did they tolerate knowing so little about what actually went on in our lives in the children's house? How did young mothers agree to part from their newborns the day they came home from the hospital?

Utopian dreams, leavened with not-so-subtle ideological coercion, made it possible for our parents to raise us this way. Their escape from Europe played a part as well. The founders of the kibbutz (in 1938) had left Germany before the war, while most of the members fled Czechoslovakia after the Nazi occupation. They were the lucky few who escaped the Holocaust. They did not speak of it much, nor define themselves as "survivors," because they had not been in the camps. But my parents—and many of their comrades—did survive a perilous journey from Prague to Palestine and then deportation and imprisonment. Their idealism was, undoubtedly, propelled by the quest for survival. This mix of idealism and necessity made it possible for our parents to create a world with a unique, collective childhood. Our own magical thinking as very young children made it joyous and rousing, at least for most of us.

Boosting our own ideological fervor was the admiring gaze of a whole country. Up until the late sixties, Israel held up the kibbutz movement as the pinnacle of its achievements. We were the best of the best, in our own eyes and in our countrymen's. We may have been geographically 238 meters below sea level, but in spirit and values we believed we were on the mountaintop. We, *kibbutzniks*, had not just seen, but we had built and inhabited, the Promised Land.

This book is about my childhood on a kibbutz in the 1950s and '60s and about my parents' ideals that brought them there in the 1940s. It begins with their extraordinary journey from Europe to pre-state Israel. After escaping from Nazi-occupied Prague, barely surviving a boat trip on the Mediterranean, arriving at the shores of Palestine as illegal immigrants, and enduring exile and imprisonment in Mauritius (a remote island in the Indian Ocean), they finally reunited in 1946 and joined Kibbutz Kfar Ruppin.

Once you learn how my parents built their home in the land of their dreams, you can better appreciate my stories. They start with my early childhood, extend into my school age and teen years, and eventually lead to when, as a young adult, I left this warm nest. The stories are all based on real events. Details and conversations are mostly my creations, some recounted with embellishments, others imagined. All the "big facts" are accurate. All the small details are authentic to the time and my subjective experiences; they are not necessarily true to life, but they express the truths of my life.

My Parents'
Journey
from Prague
to Palestine

On December 10, 1939, my parents' childhood ended. My mother, Anina Vohryzek, started her diary that day, as she left Prague.

> The train is standing at the dark platform of the Masaryk train station. I was able to get to the window. Maybe the others let me take it when they saw my sad expression. But now, when I know that my family's eyes are still on me, I smile. Steam from the train momentarily obscures the group standing behind the police on the platform. I only see the three of them: Big Hoša [my mother's younger brother], trying to disguise emotion in his now so childlike face, father's agitated expression, and you, mother. Your face that day will never leave me: those despondent eyes; the tears you didn't bother to wipe. . . .
>
> I watch the three of you with a pain I've never felt before. I smile all the more encouragingly. . . . [T]hat smile is like steam rising from the ocean of tears inside of me. . . .
>
> It took a long time and the train stood still. Then it finally started moving, slowly, but with iron certitude. . . . Now my encouraging smile is unnecessary. . . . The strangling knots in my throat give way and I cry uncontrollably. . . . I slowly calm down. I clear my head of thoughts . . . and numbly stare out the window. There's nothing to see. Everything has been blacked out.

The nighttime train arrived in Bratislava before dawn. On that train, probably in the same car, was the man who would become my father, Kurt Tramer, with other *chaverim* (comrades) in the youth movement Maccabi Ha-Tza'ir ("The Young Maccabees"). They were "comrades," with all the implications of the word at the time—comrades-in-arms set to become *chalutzim* (pioneers) on a kibbutz in Eretz Yisrael, the Land of Israel—friends, and partners in a close-knit group sharing ideological fervor, Zionist dreams, a vision of a utopian community they would build on a kibbutz in Palestine, and, occasionally, romances.

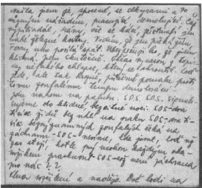

The cover and a page from the diary of my mother,
Anina Vohryzek.

My parents, traveling with sixteen other chaverim, were not yet a couple. At nineteen, a year older and a movement leader, Kurt was completely out of reach for Anina's romantic affections. Both had left their families behind: my mother, her parents and brother; my father, an only child, his divorced mother and two aunts who had raised him together.

December fifteenth was my mother's eighteenth birthday, her first one away from home. She "celebrated" with her friends on the hard floor that was her bed in a detention facility in Bratislava. She had no inkling that the promised brief sojourn to prepare documents and permits for sailing down the Danube would turn into an eight-month internment. She writes:

> *The days are all the same. I've gotten used to sleeping on the floor, eating bad food from a mess kit, not doing anything all day except for listening to rumors about our departure . . .*
>
> *I'm getting used to the guardsmen, who, depending on their moods, can be friendly jokers, or all-powerful despots.*
>
> *My birthday is sad. . . . I got two letters from home, but it only made me sadder. I miss them so.*

It was "thanks" to Adolf Eichmann's master plan for Jewish emigration from the Reich that my parents took the train from Prague to Bratislava. The Nazis had launched a "Back to the Homeland" (*Heim Ins Reich*) campaign, transporting ethnic Germans (some willingly, some not) from Eastern Europe and the Balkans up the Danube back to Germany. Eichmann allowed as many Jews as the boats could hold to travel downstream to the Black Sea—three for the price of one—thus getting rid of thousands of Jews. (My parents' transport included 3,600 Czech, Polish, and Austrian Jews.) Hefty sums were collected that more than covered the cost of the up-river journey. The Jewish emigration would stir up trouble for the British in Palestine, because the refugees had no entry certificates and would try infiltrating Palestine surreptitiously.

Eichmann actually interviewed my father regarding his application. Asked what he intended to be in Palestine, my father said, "A farmer." "Show me your hands," Eichmann ordered. "Those aren't the hands of a farmer," he said dismissively. My father froze. He'd been found out. Despite a summer of farm training (*hachsharah*), he was a city boy, a typical young Prague Jew from a lower-middle-class family, harboring intellectual aspirations. If his application were denied he'd be marooned in Prague. There were almost no other exit options. He did not dare lick his dry lips. He couldn't say a word.

"A farmer, you're sure?" Eichmann stared him down.

"A farmer . . . yes," my father managed to answer.

"Your problem," Eichmann muttered and stamped the application.

* * *

My mother came from a comfortably middle-class, highly cultured family. Jacob Cohen, her father, was a self-made, well-respected lawyer. His parents had died when he was ten, and a religious uncle took him in, grooming him to become a rabbi. When, at fourteen, Jacob

Above, Anina Vohryzek, age three or four, with her mother, Maria, and, *right*, with her father, Jacob.

rejected the yeshiva, his uncle threw him out of the house. Maria Vohryzek, my maternal grandmother, was one of seven siblings in a traditional Jewish family. The family moved to Prague during Maria's childhood but still harkened to their country home in Bohemia. I imagine that Jacob and Maria (probably called Miriam at home) met at the university. When they married in 1919, Jacob took Maria's last name, Vohryzek, worried that "Cohen" invited anti-Semitism.

My mother was doted on, along with her younger brother. Maria was unconventional and ahead of her times, insisting on fresh vegetables and fresh air. Both parents raised her with humanistic, egalitarian values and broad cultural horizons (Max Brod was an acquaintance), on occasion with some strain. Once, on a stroll one Sunday, little Anina and her father passed a street corner where prostitutes awaited customers. My mother greeted one of them warmly and received a broad smile back. Jacob hid his horror, tipping his hat as any gentlemen would in other circumstances. Later he inquired about the hearty greeting. A week before, Anina explained, the lady had offered her shelter under her umbrella during a sudden downpour. Since then, she explained, they had been friends.

Left, my father, Kurt Tramer, and his father, Josef, circa 1924. *Right*, my father's mother, Berta Gutman, in the 1920s.

"Do you know why she's on the street at this spot?" Jacob asked gingerly.

"Oh, sure! She also thinks fresh air is very important, just like Mama says."

Jacob swallowed hard and refrained from enlightening her. Instead, he increased her allowance and told her to take the tram on rainy days.

My father was a lone and lonely child, raised by his mother and her intrusive older sisters. He was born on December 16, 1920, exactly 364 days ahead of my mother, in Ostrava, about 370 kilometers due east of Prague, near the Czech-Polish border. His father, Josef Tramer, was a bon vivant. He moved his wife, Berta Gutman, and little Kurtichku—my father—to Prague in 1924. Shortly thereafter he divorced Berta, going on to marry six well-to-do widows, divorcing each one after he had run through most of her fortune to support his lifestyle. After divorcing Berta, Josef floated in and out of Kurt's young life. Sometimes he would come visit in a shiny limousine and take my father to a fancy café for decadent cream cakes. Other times he'd arrive on foot without enough change in his pocket for an ice-cream cone.

* * *

Both my parents found their passion and deepest friendships as teenagers in Maccabi Ha-Tza'ir, committed to Zionism and kibbutz ideology. For the Vohryzeks, it was all good, healthy fun. They reacted to the declared goal of moving to Palestine to be a pioneer on a kibbutz with a forgiving smile: "Yes, possibly . . . after you finish your university education." My mother was fervent about the ideals but, at the same time, also chose Maccabi Ha-Tza'ir over several other youth movements vying for the Jewish youth of Europe, because "the boys were better looking."

Left, my father's official twelfth-grade photo.[1] *Right*, my mother in summer 1939.

My father's family probably never noticed his politics or ideology.

---

1. My father is wearing a pin on his lapel with the letter gimel in Hebrew, representing his youth movement group, an act his friends considered defiant and courageous.

By age thirteen he was mostly on his own, using his modest allowance to impress his comrades by ordering black coffee and a hard-boiled egg in popular cafes. Those, he explained, were the cheapest items on the menu and quite filling. He quickly rose in the movement ranks from group counselor to coordinator of the Prague chapter. He participated in the farm *hachsharah* a year ahead of his cohort, making him, in my mother's eyes, a demigod. He was also exotically handsome: dark brown eyes, almost-black curly hair, and the dreamy air of a visionary. Girls vied for his attention (he and his father were, perhaps, more alike than he'd ever care to admit). My mother admired him from afar. She knew nothing of his great insecurity and anguish. He was hopelessly torn between two girlfriends, Kiki and Renate. Neither one joined the group on *aliyah* (immigration to Palestine). When the train departed Prague on December tenth he had to freeze those loves.

As youth movement members, my parents had a big advantage in competing for emigration slots. The Jewish community worked with Berthold Storfer, a prominent businessman and financier (a Jew who converted, yet died in Auschwitz in 1944). He negotiated with Eichmann and prepared lists of names based on age, ability to pay, fitness for work in Palestine, affiliation with a Zionist movement, and degree of danger (the latter applied to refugees from Danzig).

* * *

In Bratislava they were housed in "The Patronka"—an idle munitions factory where the acrid smell of gunpowder still hung in the air. On January 1, 1940, my mother wrote: "What happy new year? With the prospects we have? How much longer are we going to be here? The Danube has frozen over." The only good news she had was that her younger brother, Hoša, had just been spirited out of Prague by a Swedish woman, a Quaker who had organized her own "mini Kindertransport." He was safe with a family in Sweden.

My mother's younger brother, Josef (aka Hoša and Pepik), age fourteen in Prague, before departing for Sweden.

She imagined her parents—forlorn without their children but relieved that their children were safe—frantically trying to find a way out themselves. They were studying Spanish, hoping to get a visa to Argentina. They never did.

My parents were now doomed to frigid months in Bratislava until the spring thaw. Living conditions were terrible, with forty beds for eighty women, meager food rations, and the constant bickering that occurs in close quarters. Even within the intimate circle of their group—the *kvutzah*—tensions rose, chipping away at my mother's idealism: "Does the ideal I've set as my goal even exist? I never really believed in it deep down, but I considered it a weakness on my part. . . . Everyone, in their own way, has a little egotist in them."

Three months of incarceration in Bratislava went by as negotiations with the Germans dragged on. In late February my mother gloried in two weeks of relief. Her new boyfriend, Ferry, ten years older and savvier, secured passes to visit relatives in Slovakia. She was not sure about him yet: "I don't know Ferry that well. My relationship with him is uncertain. . . . [He] seems so experienced and developed compared to our boys. . . ." She went anyway, and cherished feeling "free for the first time in a long while." But when she returned there was a price to pay: "The boys from the chaverut are very cold to me and show me that they don't like how my confidence is growing and that I associate with people who are much older than they are." This was my mother's first (but not last) disappointment in the idealism of the group. They had constituted themselves as a mini-kibbutz, pooling and sharing their money, and trying to live by the principle "to each according to his needs; from each according to her abilities." The group needs were to override individual desires, and solidarity was to guide them in every step. For the first time, presaging many future occurrences on the kibbutz, my mother went against the grain of the group's ethos.

Spring became summer, the Danube had thawed long ago, but they were still waiting. Finally, on September 3, they boarded a riverboat, the *Helios*:

> *They're calling my number and I drag my luggage down. . . .*
> *I'm a little emotional to finally be leaving that dirty yard with its*
> *trashy landscape. I spent nine turbulent months of my life here. . . .*
> *The customs official confiscates a kilo of sugar, coffee, tea,*
> *cocoa, nuts, and soap from among my belongings.*
> *In the morning, at 6 a.m., the Helios raises anchor and we're*
> *off. So we're finally, really leaving!*

Four riverboats, required by the Germans to sail under swastika banners, ferried the 3,600 Jewish refugees, who, despite the beauty of the river, the lush green fields, and the crimson evening sky, all grieved for the Europe of their childhood, gone forever.[2]

---

2. See page 12 for a map showing the journey of the riverboat *Helios* from Bratislava to Tulcea. This and the other two maps (see pages 14 and 26) were hand-drawn (most likely from memory, as it's unclear if the refugees had access to an atlas) by a detainee

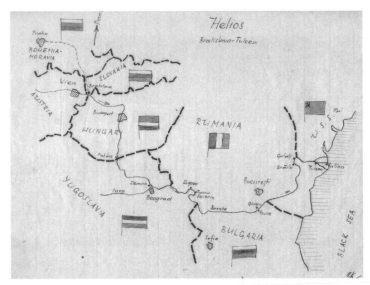

A map drawn from memory by a detainee identified only as RK.
It shows the route of the SS *Helios* from Bratislava to Tulcea.

* * *

Ten days after departing Bratislava,[3] my parents' riverboat arrived in Tulcea, on the Romanian Danube delta. In the port, my mother was excited: "We can see three ships with Panamanian flags and markings that carry the exalted names of *Atlantic, Milos,* and *Pacific.* They are far enough away, but we can see they are still being worked on." Soon the excitement evaporated: "I see the *Atlantic* up close—an old,

---

identified only as RK. The maps were bound in a booklet, written in German by Dr. A. Zwergbaum, recounting the journey from Europe to Palestine and then to Mauritius. Also included were a drawing of the SS *Atlantic* (see page 13) and a woodcut of the men's prison in Mauritius (see page 31). The booklet was typed in multiple copies using carbon paper and bound in the prison camp's book bindery in 1941. It was evidently given to my mother for her birthday, as she signed it, "Anina Vohryzkova, 15.XII.1941 Mauritius." It was stashed far back on a shelf in her library at her home in Kfar Ruppin. I only found it after her death.

3. At the time, it normally took riverboats three to four days to traverse the 250 kilometers.

badly damaged, dirty, small, constantly listing ship. She's patched with nailed-on unvarnished planks."

The next morning they boarded:

> *I think this may be the worst day of my life. . . . I can't get up the courage to go there. I'm sitting on the nearly empty deck . . . looking at that wreck; that suicide ship—with more than 1,800 people crammed on board. . . . I'm absolutely sure that boarding that ship is a . . . death sentence. Mother, Father, I'm so hopeless. Why do I have to enter that horrible, shrieking hell?*

My mother may have been the last person to board the SS *Atlantic*. It was so crowded and dark, and she was so distraught, that someone had to lead her by the hand. My father was already on board and, with other young men, had organized a leadership group—*Hanhagah*—and taken charge in the chaos. They set up food distribution, water

A drawing of the SS *Atlantic* done by a fellow passenger named Gustav Spatzier.

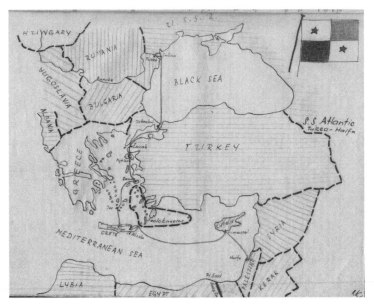

A hand-drawn map by RK showing the route of the SS *Atlantic*
from Tulcea to Palestine.

stations, and a system for using the toilets, which were merely a long
plank with holes, cantilevered off the side of the boat, and fabric parti-
tions providing minimal privacy. Single-file, passengers were to
approach the privies from the aft and depart towards the bow. The
boys' efficiency and air of confidence was reassuring, but alone at
night, my mother confessed that she was "terrified to the core of my
soul."

"Home" was now the ship's hold:

> [There are] beds made of planks that have been hammered
> together, stacked three on top of one another, just wide enough to
> sleep on. I have the top bunk, which is lucky because there is a
> light bulb that shines—a weak and sallow light, but at least it's
> there. I strain to climb over the others' heads to my spot. "Be
> careful not to touch the wire to the light. It's not insulated. . . ."
> I lie down on a dirty, prickly, awful straw mattress. It's difficult
> to breathe. . . . The boys get rid of the mattresses to gain 10
> centimeters of space and 10 more centimeters of air. [The bed]

could also be called a coffin. . . . I lie down and cry, ceaselessly;
quietly sobbing for a long time.

The *Atlantic* flies Panama's flag—in a pitiful hope of safety as a
vessel of a neutral country. Surely, no one would be fooled. It did,
however, provide some levity to the daily drudgery: going to the stern
was "a trip to Panama," and the medical clinic was "The Panama
Room."

The medical clinic was completely inadequate for the flood of sick
passengers that soon began, so only the worst cases were admitted.

Above, the
improvised hospital
called "The Panama
Room" aboard the
SS *Atlantic*.
Left, a "Hanhagah"
member standing on
guard duty on deck.

Staffing, however, was not a problem: five doctors and at least as many nurses from among the refugees reported for duty. Even before they left Tulcea, the "hospital" filled up, mostly with elderly passengers and infants. But my mother's friend was there too.

> I care for Mushi for several nights; Mushi, who I so admired at the boarding house [in Bratislava] for her intelligence, energy, and the grace that she used to overcome awful and demeaning situations. Mushi . . . was so devastated by the first day on the Atlantic that she attempted suicide. She is still unconscious, and seems to have painful hallucinations, often desperately screaming for her little girl.

Thanks to the medical care, Mushi survived.

The sail on the Black Sea was fairly calm despite the ship's tendency to list to one side. Often a Hanhagah member called out on a megaphone: "Move to the left side," and, "That's enough!" to try to keep the *Atlantic* on an even keel. Almost everyone was seasick. But the views were stunning. Istanbul was "like a fairy-tale white-gold city on the backdrop of a bright blue sunny sky: the white mosques, the *Hagia Sofia*, the beautiful palaces, thousands of spires."

On October twelfth they passed through the Dardanelles and were truly at sea. They sailed past numerous Greek islands, which, "If it were only a painting, it would be a kitschy calendar picture of blue sky, green sea, white houses, and green palm trees. In real life, it's beautiful, clear, and harmonic." When they stopped to load up coal the Greek crew refused to haul it. So "our boys go to work. They drag sacks of coal and lift them up on a rope through the air duct into the boiler room. Everything covered in coal dust: the blankets, mess kits, eyes, mouths, beds."

Within a few days the coal nearly ran out, as did water and food. My mother relayed the deprivation nonchalantly, perhaps trying to lift her own spirits:

A woodcut by internee Beda Mayer of the deck of
the SS *Atlantic*.

*We are slowly but surely getting used to being hungry and
thirsty. Bathing in salt water is not very comfortable. The soap
doesn't dissolve and you're just as dirty as when you started. I give
up breakfast—hot tea made without real tea—and use [the hot
water] to wash my neck and clean my teeth. I still have some
cologne for my face, three drops a day.*

They now feared torpedoes and bombardments, hearing air raid
sirens from the coastline. The next day the crew revolted and refused
to keep sailing. It was too dangerous: radio transmissions announced
that Italy had declared war on Greece the previous week. The crew
sabotaged the journey by throwing most of the new coal overboard in

the dark of night. At dawn, the passengers discovered this, and that most of the crew had slipped away in lifeboats. The Hanhagah "arrests the captain and locks him in his quarter. . . . [He is] removed from his post and replaced by First Officer da Costa [the only Greek sailor supportive of their cause]." Now "our boys are going into the boiler room. . . . Kurt, Dolfa, Heinz, Robert, and Gideon" were to run the boat.

When the coal ran out the passengers dismantled the boat's interior: "Everything wooden is being torn up: floors, walls, cabins, chairs, railings, planks, columns, poles; everything is being taken down. There are chains of people everywhere moving each plank hand-to-hand to the boiler room." They even burn the piano, stuck in a corner of the lounge from the boat's better days.

That night, my father faced near-ruin. As he recounted later, in a short story he wrote in 1945:

> *Trembling and fretful I walked down . . . half asleep and frightened. . . .*
>
> *The heat was awful. I reluctantly got hold of a bucket, filled it with water and poured [it] on the heap [of ashes]. But near, too near, was I standing to it and a blast of dirty, sizzling vapor exploded into my face. I stumbled, the bucket fell down and I ran, covering my face, to the ship's hospital. There, on the door of it, I collapsed, unconscious.*

He spent two weeks in the Panama Room, "my face completely bandaged with holes for my eyes and mouth." The doctors changed his bandages daily and warned him not to touch them. When he asked for the truth about his prognosis, they said they could not know.

> *—the feared, dreadful truth was clear. My face was to be a monster's . . . my imagination fired up by films like "the Phantom of the Opera," went into work. . . . So I got hold of poison, I mean, I always had a little capsule with me since Hitler came to my*

town. I looked at it . . . wondering how, in such a small trifle like this . . . the fate of a man can be condemned.

Miraculously, when the bandages were removed his face was fine: "reddish, wrinkled—but undistorted, whole, clean—my old face!"

* * *

The boat now floated at the mercy of currents and wind. There was nothing left to feed the engines. Finally, after repeated SOS signals were broadcast "out into the calm, unfeeling night," it seemed their luck had turned. My mother writes:

> *A wave of emotion and hope: two ships on the horizon. S.O.S. Do they see us? Italians? English? They're answering! They're coming closer! It's two English cruisers.*
> *Costu signals that we're in grave danger, without coal, without water, without supplies, using the wood for fuel. We tensely wait for an answer. . . . "We are sorry but can't help" and they leave.*

* * *

At dawn, after two more days without food and water, they saw land. Where were they? It could have been Turkey, Palestine (could they be that lucky?), Egypt, or, God forbid, Nazi-allied Italy or Libya. The passengers strained to glimpse an identifying landmark. They saw nothing definitive—just a typical Mediterranean coastline. Anxiety was so high that there was utter silence.

My mother got ready to meet her fate: "I put some photos, three letters from home, documents, addresses, and the keys to my locker in a waterproof pouch around my neck."[4]

---

4. While still in Prague, my mother had packed and shipped a trunk with "essentials" to Palestine, to be collected at the Haifa port when she arrived. When my mother finally

A motorboat approaches from the shore. We're packed against
the remnants of the railing trying to make out a flag—joy breaks
loose—a Union Jack. . . . There is a clear rainbow above our
heads. Is that a symbol? We laugh like fools with tears in our eyes,
and we don't even think about being an illegal transport in the
hands of the English. . . . We only know that we're free of that
horrible uncertainty. We're saved.

Mother, Father, do you hear? A rainbow above us; I will see
you again.

A British tugboat towed the *Atlantic* into Limassol (Cyprus), one
of the busiest Mediterranean ports deployed in the war effort. The
British quickly discovered that they were Jews intent on entering Palestine illegally. The British remained mum on the refugees' fate.
They loaded food, water, medicine, and coal onto the boat, "all for a
fee, of course. Yes, but we don't have money. We start a collection.
. . . The authorities are accommodating. . . . [T]hey accept . . . other
valuables: wedding rings, medical kits, pens, watches, and the like."

On November 23, after eleven days in Limassol, no longer hungry
and parched but still afflicted by a typhoid epidemic and fearful for
their future, they set sail for Palestine.

We're off . . . the last part of the journey! We don't sleep at
night, so we can see the shores of Eretz Yisrael.

At 4:15 we see a distant gray line of Syrian mountains as the
sun rises. . . . We cannot tear our gaze away from the land in
front of us. We sing the happiest, most thoughtful version of
Hatikva and Techezakna.⁵ . . . We're consumed by happiness. It

---

claimed it in August 1945, it had been vandalized and was half empty. In light of that, the
British port officer waived the five-year "holding fee" she would have had to pay.

5. Chaim Nachman Bialik's popular song celebrating the chalutzim.

was not all in vain. Despite the suffering of the journey we have reached our goal!

They entered Haifa harbor, anchoring two hundred yards from the dock.

We learn that we will be transferred to the Patria, a beautiful, new, four-deck ocean liner where the people from the Milos and the Pacific are already waiting, [6] *allegedly because we will only be under quarantine a short time.*

It seemed logical and innocuous. Some even praised the British for their orderly handling of the situation, so reassuring after their chaotic journey. They were to be transferred to the SS *Patria* the next morning, and were advised to get some much-needed sleep.

Just after 9:00 a.m. on the morning of November 25, my mother and her comrades stood at the ready, with approximately 1,500 other *Atlantic* passengers. Families with young children, the elderly, and the sick, had already made the short passage on small 25-person dinghies to the *Patria*. Among them—as my mother recounted in a memoir written over seventy years later—was her high school friend Gertie, a champion swimmer from Prague. Gertie had promised my mother and her friend Ruth to secure them good spots. My mother waved to a speck on the *Patria's* deck, perhaps Gertie. She turned to tell Ruth something, when "a thunderous noise and the *Patria* starts to lean, and lean, and turn over on its side." In seconds, she recounts, the *Patria* was half sunk.

As vivid as her description is, it is faulty. In fact, the *Patria* sank slowly, almost gracefully, taking twelve minutes to come to rest on its side. Its three chimneystacks jutted diagonally out of the water. The *Patria's* wreck remained there for months, perhaps years, settling

---

6. These were the two boats that left Tulcea with them but that had arrived two weeks earlier.

The SS *Patria* sinking in the Haifa harbor. Courtesy of the Ghetto Fighters' House Museum Archive, Israel.

down onto the harbor floor at an imperceptibly slow pace, to serve as a deterrent to future attempts at illegal immigration: "Behold and beware."

The passengers on the *Atlantic* were petrified. The motorboats that had just set out towards the *Patria* returned: "The people on our ship are pale, terrified. They aren't able to speak." Everyone on the *Atlantic* watched British vessels and, soon, Arab fishermen as well, approach the *Patria* to pull survivors out of the water. The vessels could not get close to the sinking ship: its body and the cargo tumbling off the deck created dangerous vortexes that could suck one under water.

Almost immediately "there are rumors about the reasons for the disaster: Arab sabotage . . . an explosion in the engine room . . ." In the following days the passengers learned that the *Patria* had not been intended as temporary quarantine. Rather, it was to have deported them—a total of 3,600 refugees from the *Atlantic, Pacific,* and *Milos*—to Mauritius, a British colony island in the Indian Ocean. Only in 1957 did Munia Mardor, a member of the paramilitary pre-state group Haganah, reveal the truth about the *Patria*. Determined to prevent the deportation to Mauritius after negotiations with the Mandate authorities had failed, the Haganah resorted to sabotage.

By 9:15 am, November 25, there were about two hundred "*Atlantics*" on the *Patria*. They had not heard the order to assemble on deck. Most were busy in the ship's belly, finding beds and nooks to stow their luggage. When the explosion ripped off the *Patria's* side, water gushed in and flooded the interior, trapping most of them. With a huge shudder, the *Patria* keeled over and began sinking. Hundreds of passengers on deck were thrown off into the water. The lucky ones avoided the falling cargo and swirling vortexes, and managed to swim to the dock. Most of the passengers seized railings, masts, bollards, and ropes, holding on until eventually rescued. Approximately 260 drowned, many of them *Atlantic* passengers trapped in lower cabins. Among the drowned were about fifty British police and soldiers, one of them reportedly sacrificing his life to rush to the engine room to turn off the remaining boilers and release the steam. Most of the bodies were trapped in the bowels of the ship and never recovered.

* * *

That catastrophic day ended with the *Patria* survivors being bused to Atlit, a large detention camp south of Haifa, while hundreds of wounded went to hospitals in Haifa (once recovered, they were sent to Atlit). The 1,500 passengers still on the *Atlantic* were sent to Atlit as well. My mother writes:

> *I see a two-meter-high wall with barbed wire. My emotions freeze. . . . I can't describe that mix of feelings. We walk down a street between two rows of buildings behind barbed wire, which stabs me to the soul.*

They were ordered into barracks, each housing forty people: "There are two blankets on the beds; all the same, new, brown, with a big PP—Palestine Police—on them. There aren't enough beds. We have to sleep three to every two [beds]."

They asked about other friends who had been on the *Patria*. The answer was, "They aren't here yet, but we hope . . ." My mother was skeptical. Hundreds were missing: "Mothers are looking for children, children looking for parents, brothers for sisters; they keep asking and every 'no' plunges them further down into hopelessness." Gertie was never found; the champion swimmer had drowned.

* * *

On December 5th the camp was abuzz: the survivors of the *Patria* would be allowed to remain in Palestine legally. Churchill had overruled Sir Harold MacMichael, the Palestine high commissioner, citing an age-old international convention that guarantees shipwreck survivors safe haven at the nearest shore. The *Patria* survivors were jubilant. Across the road the "*Atlantics*" were crushed. Rumors spread instantly that they would be deported, and very soon. But there was no official word from the British, and the *ghaffirs* (Jewish policemen and women) only said, "Stay strong, the whole Yishuv is behind you."[7]

On December 8th the commandant announced: the *Atlantics* will depart at midnight. At first there was utter disbelief and despair, but soon the refugees organized "for passive resistance. Everyone in the camp will strip naked and lie in their beds. No one will move in response to any requests or orders, or violence. We strip and lie down." It was to no avail. At night the police arrived in great force and systematically beat the mostly-naked men. They dragged them onto trucks. Screams and shouts rang through the camp. Officers entered the women's barracks every half hour and barked orders. No one moved. At daybreak the police barged in and threw blankets over the naked women, ordering, "Cover up! Pack up!"

---

7. The pre-state Jewish community in Palestine.

We exit the gate and there are covered buses waiting on the road. We get on. I stare at a row of tall palm trees so intently I start to cry. I will remember that image until my death: A soldier with a truncheon in front of a row of tall palms, a blue sky, and behind me cries and curses.

On the bus,

The soldier next to me offers me cigarettes. I give him an awful look. He looks embarrassed and sad. In a halting voice he says: "But it's not my fault. It's my obligation. I have two children." He has tears in his eyes. Suddenly, I feel sorry for him, too. He gives me a piece of paper and a pen. "Write. I'll be certain to send it."

I waver. Then I write down the Arnsteins' [relatives in Haifa] address: "Write to parents via Hoša. Healthy. Anina."

All she could write was "healthy." The Arnsteins would read about her fate in the papers. By then it would be too late: the ship deporting them would have already sailed.

The buses passed Haifa's nearly empty streets. The refugees were despondent. The promise "The whole Yishuv is behind you" rang hollow. There were no mass demonstrations to try to stop their expulsion. The view of the sea opened up. My mother told her friend Lily: "And we celebrated that it can't hurt us anymore."

* * *

Two large ships anchored in Haifa's port: the SS *New Zealand* and the SS *Johann de Witt*, with Dutch crews at the helm. The refugees embarked: my mother and her female friends onto the *New Zealand*, my father, Ferry, and most of the "boys" onto the *Johann de Witt*. They set sail side by side to the Suez Canal, down to Aden, along the coast of East Africa, and into the Indian Ocean. It was heaven compared to the *Atlantic*. "The food is wonderful: butter, meat, cheese, desserts."

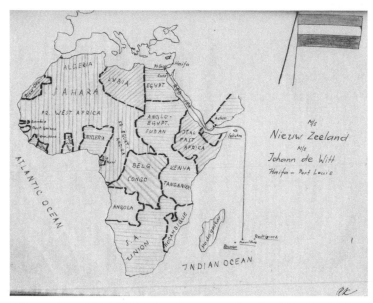

A map drawn by RK showing the route taken by the refugees on
two ships, the SS *New Zealand* and the SS *Johann de Witt*,
from Palestine to Mauritius.

At first many passengers fell ill from overeating. They got cigarettes
and fresh fruit from the English policemen guarding them. Some of
the women flirted with them and got extra portions and treats. Some,
my mother is certain, offered more. The policemen were not embarrassed to solicit.

On December 15 she was somewhere in the Indian Ocean:

> *Today is my birthday, so I have another reason to be sad. This
> is my second one without my parents. Not even Ferry is here. Lily
> gave me a handkerchief and a cigarette case that she received from
> her mother and was very important to her. . . . Bibi found three
> cigarettes somewhere. Various people put together two and a half
> cigarettes; a real treasure.*

The 3,900 nautical miles voyage to the island of Mauritius, seven
hundred miles due east of Madagascar, took three weeks. Every day

of southward movement it got hotter and muggier. The passengers sweated with the smallest effort and anxiously awaited what they would find on this *terra incognita*. It's the rare year when Hanukkah and Christmas fall on the same day. The refugees lighted the first candle while in the midst of the tropics, many pining for snow-covered Prague or Vienna.

The next day they saw land on the horizon: a mountain range covered in lush green vegetation. Their spirits lifted.

> *We anchor during sunset several kilometers from Port Louis. We stand on the deck as though in shock. The view is incredibly beautiful. A lightly choppy sea, as azure as the sky, which has hues of red from the setting sun; mountains scattered with peaks and cliffs and a wealth of vegetation. We can see lights on shore; see cars and hear horns. It's not a wild desert! From this view, [it seems like] a civilized island paradise.*

To their amazement, they got a tremendous welcome:

> *The road is lined with beautiful trees, gorgeous blossoms, palm trees, cacti, and sugar cane fields . . . and flocks of tiny colorful children that call, wave, jump, and throw flowers into our path. . . . [T]he Chinese, the blacks, the creoles, the Indians, all express their welcoming of us: "Bienvenue mesdames les réfugiées, messieurs les réfugiés!"*[8]

Next, almost a miracle:

> *A large sign advertising Bat'a [a Czech shoe manufacturer with many international branches] sends us into a frenzy . . . it's almost the same as at home!*

---

8. Recounted in my mother's memoir, composed in her late eighties.

But the pleasant surprise evaporated when the bus halted "in front of a large stone building with huge, closed gates—His Majesty's prison." Suddenly they fully understood: they were prisoners now. The main part was a massive basalt building erected by Napoleon for his political prisoners. The men would be housed there. Adjacent was a hastily constructed compound of wooden huts with corrugated tin roofs for the women. A lone gate connected the two camps. "The view in front of us is like a punch in the belly. It looks desperate. . . . From today on I am detainee number 699." My mother entered her hut—its only distinction was the letter R on the front. "Inside there is a wooden floor and 30 beds, and nothing else. Each of us sits on one bed. Live here? How?"

After dinner in the mess hall, the prisoners reported their names and shoe sizes, and received sheets and mosquito nets. The women were allowed to enter the men's side to try to find husbands, brothers, and friends. "I see Ferry. I barely recognize him. He's wearing dark pajama pants and has a mustache. My first words . . . are rather stupid: 'For God's sake, shave that off!'"

My father was in the men's camp, too, presumably without an objectionable moustache. My mother didn't mention him by name but was clearly relieved to locate all the "boys" from the group. A few days later the refugees' luggage arrived "in mostly terrible condition: dirty, tattered, and knocked about. The most valuable things are missing." My mother hunted for her possessions, but

The cigarette case with the Czechoslovak Republic emblem is . . . gone. The Primus [kerosene stove], Allegro [fountain pen], money, addresses—it's all gone. . . . Ferry cannot find his iron toolbox.

Ferry had carried his toolbox since Bratislava and "never let it out of his sight," a subject of persistent friendly mocking by the group. Now my mother learned why: "Only now he tells me that one of the wrenches was made of gold [disguised with black paint]. The price it could fetch could support us for a year."

* * *

Life in Mauritius was harsh. Initially the greatest hardships were adjusting to the local water and food, the intense heat and mosquitos, and the torrential downpours. In the women's barracks the noise was relentless, whether from the pounding rain hammering on tin roofs or women "constantly quarreling." Gradually the detainees developed daily activities, establishing a school and setting up workshops for carpentry (where my father learned the craft), metalworking, sewing, and doll making. The refugees adopted the British officials' slogan: "Keep the people busy."

Forthwith, people fell ill with serious diseases: malaria, typhus, and virulent infections of any open wound. In the first three months over forty refugees died. My mother and her friend Lily volunteered to be nursing aides in the hospital that the British established for the detainees. Refugee doctors and nurses served as medical staff alongside British personnel. Local Mauritians were orderlies, cooks, and janitors.

My mother in her nurse's uniform in Mauritius.

January 15, 1941

We finally got our orders and at 10 tonight Lily and I are to start the night shift in the women's typhoid ward. . . . We're nervous because we have no idea what goes on there and what we're supposed to do. . . .

The ward is lit by a damped light, with 57 beds: cries, sighs, calls, tears, babble, unconscious screaming, begging, curses, beseeching, and prayers. "Trinken, Hilfe, Schuessel, Durst. Schwester, Schwester!" ("Drink, Help, Urinal, Thirst. Nurse, Nurse!"). It grinds itself into our terrified souls. . . .

At six in morning, they come to relieve us, thank God. . . . I fall into bed, but I'm so tired, I can't fall asleep.

Not surprisingly, within a fortnight my mother was sick herself: severe bronchitis with high fever. She was hospitalized for twelve days until "I'm finally going home, or, better put, they're carrying me on a stretcher. After lying down for so long, I can't walk yet. My legs are like spilled toothpicks and I get dizzy." A week later she was back on duty at the hospital where Ferry, too, was now working as an aide.

The death toll mounted. All told, 128 refugees died in Mauritius and were buried in a Jewish section of the St. Martin Cemetery. Many were elderly, but not all. My mother was in anguish when a seven-year-old girl died and, later, when a young man succumbed to typhoid:

February 25, 1941

This night was terrible. Five people died; three women and two men. Joži Marode, 20, a happy, friendly boy from Vienna. He lay unconscious for days, then suddenly improved; usually a fateful sign. Today, as he died . . . in agony, he sang utterly beautifully, and hopelessly sadly. "Wien, Wien nur du allein . . ." ("Vienna, Vienna, you alone"), and he died . . .

* * *

A woodcut of the interior of the men's prison in
Mauritius by internee Beda Mayer.

Time crawled like the giant tortoise that once roamed the island.
Four months passed without a diary entry. On August 26 my mother
writes: "A four-month gap. I can't write. Nothing happens or changes."
As time went by, many initiatives sprang up. One fellow who had a
Primus kerosene stove (my mother never found hers) set up a café.
He boiled water and served people (they had to bring their own cup),
encouraging them to imagine their wish—coffee or tea—and con-
verse as they would in a proper coffee house. Tea eventually arrived,
as they were, after all, in the British Empire where it's a fundamental
life necessity. Coffee was ersatz—made from burnt barley. In addition to craft workshops, the detainees cultivated a vegetable garden,

where they honed their skills preparing for their dream of working the land on a kibbutz. They created a robust cultural life as well, setting up a theatre troupe, an orchestra, and a choir. In January 1941 the South African Jewish community received their letter requesting assistance, including clothing, medical supplies, books and paper, ritual articles, sports equipment and games, and the following musical instruments: "1 piano, 2 saxophones, 2 clarinets, 1 viola, as many violins and guitars as possible, strings and bows for the instruments and sheet music for classical and Jazz."

Some detainees put on a theatrical revue of such quality that it was "performed for an audience from the city, and three times for the camp." They also performed Puccini's *La Bohème* (joined by some local, less accomplished, talent) in the Port Louis Opera House. For my parents and their Maccabi Ha-Tza'ir comrades, this was just a rehearsal, albeit in extremis, for the idealistic and culturally vibrant community they planned to establish in the kibbutz of their dreams. In 1944 some songs from the theatrical productions were "published" in a carbon-copied, typed, and hand-bound booklet titled "Anu Olim Artza" (We Are Immigrating to Our Homeland). My mother saved one as a souvenir.[9]

But moments of celebration were rare. Material deprivation, illnesses, and—surely the worst—complete ignorance of the fate of their families in Europe and hopelessness about an end to their own exile took a heavy toll. Many were despondent and apathetic; a few committed suicide.

* * *

---

9. After my mother died I found the booklet in the back of the bookcase, along with other Mauritius publications: an accounting of their journey from Europe (in German, by Dr. Aren Zwergbaum, one of the refugees' leaders) with stunning woodcuts depicting the Atlantic and the prison in Mauritius, and a report to a British Colonial Office representative who visited in 1943, detailing their unsuitable living conditions and grievances.

In September 1941 my mother was lucky to survive acute appendicitis. Going into surgery, "I didn't feel a speck of fear as I was falling asleep. But I did when I awoke . . . sick from the chloroform. I kept calling out for mother. Then I remembered that I'm on Mauritius." She was glad to return "home" to the camp, where, a week later, there was stunning news: the Czech young men would be permitted to volunteer for the British Army, to serve in the "Czech Free Army." Her comrades, "Kurtichek [my father], Dolfa, Robert, Šimonek, Erich, Gideon, and all the others" would soon leave. She admitted that, in secret, she hoped nothing would come of it. Ferry was skeptical and decided against volunteering.

On December 15, her third birthday away from home, she tried to cheer herself: "I received many presents; so much that I was a bit embarrassed. The most beautiful was the telegram Ferry (said he) sent to my parents through Switzerland." She was thrilled but, clearly, had doubts, putting "said he" in parenthesis. She'd had no news from her parents at all; a telegram via Switzerland seemed dubious.

Nor had my father had any contact with his family. Unbeknownst to him, in November 1941 his mother, Berta, was still in Prague (having evaded the first transports of Prague Jews to Lodz) and wrote to her brother, Edwin, in Chicago: "Kurt is now in Port Louis, P.O.B. / Postfach/1000/Mauritius." In February 1942 my father sent a Red Cross telegram to "Renate, Rudolf and Mutter" in Prague,[10] asking about their welfare. It arrived on May 20. Renate signed for it and added a response, sending it back to Mauritius. There it was stamped "Passed" by the local censor months late, long after my father had already departed.[11] Sometime in fall 1942, Berta, Renate, and Rudolf were deported to Terezin. After the war my father learned that Berta had died in the Czech Family Camp in Auschwitz. There, as my

---

10. Renate evidently moved in with Kurt's mother some time in 1941 or 42. Rudolf was probably Renate's husband.

11. The fact that my father had this telegram in his papers suggests it was forwarded to him at his unit in the British Army.

mother learned after the war, her father had died as well. Her mother had died earlier in the Lodz ghetto.

None of this was known on Mauritius. On April 16, 1942, watching the ship carrying the "boys" to their service in the British Army sail away, my mother's diary ends. Paradoxically, imminent separation unleashed my mother's feelings for my father. Until now, those had been bottled up. Two days before the April 16 departure, they said their farewells.

> *I visited Kurt this afternoon. He gave me his latest photograph, which was done here and it's excellent. And he gave me a picture of him at about five years old, which I liked so much. I tried, rather successfully, to speak and act as though nothing is going on.*

The next day:

> *In my mind's eye, I can see Kurt, his curly hair, his eyes, his expression. And he leaves; into uncertainty. It keeps getting worse. My heart is already in pieces for what is happening at home, where Hoša is, what will become of Kurt, and, if it must always get worse, what is yet to come?*

On the sixteenth she writes:

> *When we went to breakfast in the morning, we could see the boys walking out the back gate, one after another. They're leaving the camp, opening the walls, leaving Mauritius. They're free. Devil take my "but," my pessimism, my agitation.*
>
> *I must not, must not shed a single tear. . . .*
>
> *Three o'clock . . . We can see . . . a ship in the fog . . . constantly smaller and less visible. We can't see it anymore. The fog has swallowed it up and taken it from our eyes. But they are better off now, seeing a disappearing and shrinking Mauritius.*

"Czech Free Army" volunteers leaving the
camp in Mauritius.

There are no diary entries after this one.

⁂ ⁂ ⁂

Conditions on Mauritius continued to be harsh. A report submitted
by the detainees to a British Foreign Office delegate visiting the camp
notes that 720 men are imprisoned in eight-foot cells with no lighting, only every fifth person gets an actual bed, and others have only a
thin mat and two blankets. Over 700 women are housed in crowded
corrugated-tin barracks where summer temperatures exceed 100°F.
Food supplies, the report continues, are insufficient: the 300 grams
of meat "on the books" is generally replaced by 25 grams of beans; 40
percent of detainees have malaria, 50 percent suffer from vitamin

deficiency, 15 percent from chronic dysentery. The list goes on, citing inadequate clothing, insufficient financial resources, no formal education for children, extreme restrictions on intimate family life, Polish and Czech citizens prevented from listening to the BBC or writing their families letters in their native languages, and confiscation of passports and other identification documents.

The British eventually loosened the rules: they allowed day passes to town or the beach, as well as access to the BBC and a daily French-language Mauritian newspaper. The refugees could now learn about the state of the war in Europe and begin to hope that its end was in sight. They still had no information about the families they left in Europe. With the young men from her *kvutzah* gone, my mother eventually married Ferry in February 1943, and they took advantage of the more-frequent visits married couples were allowed to have with each other.

On an outing to town, my mother wandered past a small Buddhist temple. Curious, she entered and talked to the monk about the teachings of the Buddha. She told him about the detainees. He had no inkling of their presence nor their hair-raising escape from Europe, and didn't seem interested. My mother was shocked but her curiosity was piqued, and she visited several times, read booklets he lent her, and tried meditation. In summer 1943 she received the February 1943 issue of *Readers Digest* (sent to her by a former client of her father's living in New York) with American Jewish writer Ben Hecht's description—for the first time in the Western press—of the systematic murder of Jews in death camps. In great agitation she reported this to the monk. He brushed his palm past his face in a gesture of dismissal, as if shooing away a gnat. This world and its troubles were of no consequence in his Buddhist eyes. My mother never went back.

* * *

Meanwhile, my father and his eighty-five young Czech co-recruits had shipped off to South Africa for a short training and then to the battleground in Egypt. He was stationed in Alexandria, where his main occupation, as he would recount, chuckling, was "to sweep the sand off the desert." In fact, his skillful hands and excellent head for numbers and logistics became evident quickly, and he took charge of carpentry and metalwork shops. He learned to use a lathe and made a beautiful large plate from mahogany and a wood-inlay box. (I grew up with the plate on the wall and the box on the bookshelf, holding precious items—from my father's British Army medals to my first baby tooth.)

The Allies' victory in El Alamein in November 1942 decided the fate of the African front. My father's unit was spared combat but sustained several Luftwaffe aerial bombings. The first time, a fellow soldier jumped out of the trench screaming at the plane overhead: "Are you crazy? There're people down here!"

The unit was transferred to Palestine, and Kurt took on similar duties, overseeing material production and logistics. Sometime in 1943 the regiment received orders for deployment in Europe. My father balked. It had taken him four years to get to Palestine from

My father (*on the far left with hands on hips*) with his
army unit in Egypt.

Europe on his first try; he wasn't going back. He deserted and hid in Kibbutz Kineret on the shores of the Sea of Galilee. The military police looked for him in vain in his kibbutz, Kfar Ruppin, where they garnered no leads.

Three months later my father appeared at the British Army draft office. "There was a fire in my apartment," he explained, "so I have no identification documents. My name is Chaim Korati. I am a Palestinian Jew and I want to enlist to fight the cursed Nazis." They took him in and stationed him at Beit Naballah (in central Israel, near Ramle), a major transportation and material production hub with its own train station. Fortunately, he never ran across someone who recognized him as Kurt Tramer, a Czech Jew.

He wrote my mother two letters from Palestine, which arrived in Mauritius in 1945, near the end of her stay. He reported about all their chaverim in the British army. He had no details about the four who had been selected for the Royal Air Force and shipped to England for pilot training. Later he learned that one of them, his close friend George Morgenstern (later George Morton), began his training only to discover that he was colorblind. He was transferred to military intelligence, making good use of his fluent German. The three who became RAF pilots went out together on a bombing sortie. They never came back.

* * *

When the war in Europe ended, the Mauritius detainees anxiously awaited word of their fate. In August they learned that the Czech Free Government (seated in London in wartime) had appealed on their behalf to His Majesty's fairness and compassion. True, the British had the right to refuse entry to those Czech citizens at Palestine's shores. True, perhaps, they had the right to deport them, but, surely, not to imprison them for nearly five years. The Crown agreed, allowing the Mauritius detainees to enter Palestine legally. On August 26,

1945, after a three-week voyage, they arrived in Haifa's port, where the *Patria*'s three chimneys were no longer visible.

My mother wanted to go immediately to Kfar Ruppin to join her comrades and fulfill her long-cherished kibbutz dreams. But the Haifa-based Arnsteins convinced her that after all she'd been through, she shouldn't rush to the kibbutz at the end of the road; it was 110 degrees in August, with no fans, not much food, but abundant malaria. She should stay in Haifa for a while to "get Mauritius out of me," and experience, for the first time ever, living as a free adult. She wrote all this to Kurt and added that she and Ferry had parted amicably when the entry into Palestine was granted. He was hoping to return to Prague; he certainly had no intention of going to a kibbutz.

She recounts in her memoir:

> One day, when I'm alone in the [Arensteins'] apartment, the doorbell rings. I open. And, there, in front of me, stands a soldier in an ironed uniform, so handsome! It was Kurt. I fell in love with him on the spot, with such intensity that I can feel that moment today.

From this moment on my parents, though mostly apart for the next eleven months, were a couple. Throughout his service until July 1946, Kurt alternated between visiting my mother and going to Kfar Ruppin. My mother soon left Haifa for nursing training (she had, she realized, acquired some practical skills in Mauritius) at Afula Hospital, where my siblings and I would be born.

They began a feverish correspondence, love and passion exploding on each page.[12] In his first letter my father professed his love but also castigated himself for how tongue-tied, awkward, and self-centered he was when they met:

---

12. Less than twenty-five years later, in fall 1970, David Biale and I began a similar correspondence, first gingerly but soon growing into a full-fledged romance. After over three hundred letters we married in 1973.

When I heard the precious news of your coming to Palestine, I visualized, rehearsed and "played" our first meeting over and over again till—when its realization finally came . . . there was such a vast amount of compassion, love and warmth towards you strangled in my throat. . . .

The years we didn't see each other are a blank in my mind. . . . You are for me the dearest person I have.

But all was not rosy. My father continues:

My wish is to have a wife as intelligent as you are. . . . I doubt I'll find one as good and sincere, as friendly and compassionate as you are. But you have acquired many things you must get rid of, for your own good . . . which force that homey, battered, scared, scorched shield of yours—the shield you hold before you, defending the warm and sympathetic inner part against the cruel world . . .

He pledged to do all he could to restore her trust in humanity and, together, to rekindle their idealism.

The letters cover the gamut: from endless declarations of eternal love to details of daily life, the logistics of their next meeting, and dreams about finally joining the kibbutz. One planned meeting after another evaporated: my father's day pass was revoked, the bus never came, my mother had to fill another nurse's slot, and there was a nationwide curfew. In Afula my mother trudged, exhausted and lonely, through grinding hospital work. "This place, 'Awfulla'—is a bit of a solitary confinement."

* * *

On their few dates they were delirious with love, but also faced difficult moments: the cloud of their parents' deaths in Europe, uncertainties about their future on the kibbutz, the hardships of separation. On March 28, my father reported excitedly: "According to

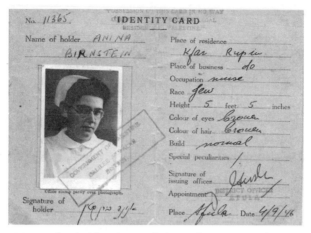

My mother's identity card, issued on September 4,
1946, under her then-married name, Birnstein.

reliable sources my release will be in January 1947 at the latest." That
was nine months away, but their fantasies about their kibbutz life
blossomed. He added: "P.S. I think I am going to make little models
of our furniture. We'll then know how it really looks."

In April my mother received her official identity card. It fell short
of her hopes for full legalization. Stamped behind the heading "Identity Card" in purple ink is written: "Possession of this card in no way
constitutes evidence of legal residence in Palestine."

Some months earlier my father had secured his legal status,
thanks to his British Army service. But when my mother congratulated him on being "respectable," he answered: "I didn't get 'respectable' by getting my legalization. On the contrary, I despise myself and
the people or forces that are responsible for such a course being
taken and necessary. But . . . it is a necessity."

Though they disdained the formalities of bourgeois marriage, my
father declared:

> We shall marry and I accept your [marriage] proposal. . . . We
> should even marry officially and have a nice little "clean"
> wedding—but that part is the same as my legalization. I accept it

as a necessity against which it is foolish to protest or worry
about—but which is essentially evil. . . . [As] workers (proletarians
even), socialist and reformers . . . our way of living is and will be
an inner and outer revolt against the world.

Would the kibbutz they so fervently dreamed of meet their ideal of
"inner and outer revolt against the world"? When my mother
expressed doubts after two visits there, Kurt exhorted: "We're overdo-
ing it. . . . We fear disappointment so much . . . hope [for] success so
desperately that we become two anxious fools. . . ." They were willing
to sacrifice much, be it material comforts or professional aspirations
(for my father, to be a carpenter, for my mother, a nurse), losing
friends who would surely leave the kibbutz, and living far from the
cultural life they cherished—classical music, theatre, museums. My
mother summed up: "I am prepared . . . [for] all that . . . giving up,
giving up, and giving up; *all except values.*"

In April 1946 my father was shipped back to Alexandria to manage a large carpentry shop. With a promised staff of thirty to forty, he
was to oversee the dismantling of British Army installations. His
demobilization was still promised by year-end, but now my parents
faced months of total separation. They wrote more frequently. Amaz-
ingly, letters from Alexandria to Afula often arrived faster than they
had within Palestine.

My father was lonely and often frustratingly inactive in Alexandria. Most of the workers promised for the carpentry shop never
materialized. He worked with German POWs who were competent,
hard workers. He found it terribly distressing:

It makes me dizzy . . . to think I might once, in an unguarded
moment, smile at one of them; and, on the other hand, I am
astonished for the satisfaction I get from the thought of how hellish
I can make their lives for a month or two if I choose. . . . As far as
I have seen . . . they seem a decent lot and damn good workers.
Oh, oh, oh, blast it!

This brief passage is one of the very few places within nearly ninety letters where my father mentions Germans. Indeed, my parents very rarely referred to Europe, the Nazis, the fate of family left behind, and reports of the scope of the Holocaust. One exception is a fraught moment in late 1945–early 1946, on a day together at Kibbutz Ginegar (near Afula).

Months later, my father wrote from Alexandria:

> *Now you will perhaps understand a little the scene in*
> *Ginegar—I was unconsciously grudging you the "pleasure" to*
> *weep over your parents . . .*[13]
>
> *I still can't realize my mother is dead. I still can't grasp the true*
> *and full meaning of it—for I never understood her rightly. . . .*
> *Sometimes it pains [me] to know I missed something in life,*
> *something very important, vital. It's like being a cripple. . . .*

Somewhat indirectly, he also mourned the murder of my mother's parents: "I should have loved to know your parents and home— for I never had a real home   I should have loved them accepting me as their son."

Mostly they wrote of longing for each other and how inadequate letters are for loving. Still, they wrote and wrote, sometimes three letters a day. On April 27, a three-letter-day, my father illustrated his frenzy with a cartoon and a poem:

> Nailed to the chair,
> and writing table . . .
>
> If I want to live and love you,
> can you blame me?

---

13. Evidently my mother had just told him that she had learned of her parents' deaths in the camps.

A cartoon, drawn by my father, of himself at his writing desk.

But good news soon turned everything around:

I'll be demobed [demobilized] at the beginning of this blessed July 1946. . . .

Darling, Aninko, how much I love you. All we dreamt about getting suddenly so close. So cheerfully close, too tangible almost . . .

They immediately started imagining building their new life. They would have a home (albeit, one room in a wooden hut); my father would build all their furniture, then children. They discussed practical matters: what can they afford to buy? Curtains, an ashtray, maybe a bedspread? Most important, a fan—"ventilator." But, my mother soon reported, "We won't have a ventilator after all. They cost at least 6.50£ [about $300 in today's currency]."

Their impending reunion stirred up unfinished business about my mother's marriage and my father's two loves in Prague. Regarding the first, my father was laconic: "Get busy on your divorce business—if possible." About his old loves he is still passionate, even if he might hurt my mother's feelings.

> *My love for you did change nothing in what I felt once towards Kiki and Renke . . .*
>
> *I wouldn't attempt to persuade you that K. and R. were "fake" and you the only "true love." Yes, I love you differently, quite differently, for we are grown up to a certain degree. But the mere intensity of feeling [for K. and R.] is unchanged.*

My mother reassured him: "I am not at all sad or anything else about Kiki and Renka [sic]. It's what I expected you to be like. I would only be sad were it less . . ." But she tread lightly. She didn't broach the dark cloud over the old loves. While Kiki had managed to escape Europe (to Ecuador and from there to the United States), Renke had remained in Prague (with Kurt's mother) and perished in the Holocaust.

On May 1 the countdown began. From now on each letter tallied the days left until July 18, the day my father expected to arrive in Afula (by train from Alexandria). "Get prepared," he warned, "for a physical shock for I'll be raving mad with love when I see you again. . . . Better meet me with a chaperone (one who is prepared to stand being thrown down stairs)." My mother answered: "Darling Kurt, do you realize, but realize, it's in 28 days? . . . My world is small in these days. . . . It's you and Eretz Yisrael."

But just as their horizons brightened, gloom and dread engulfed Eretz Yisrael. Tensions exploded in June as attacks on British forces by the Haganah, Lehi, and Etzel (aka the Irgun; the latter two were Revisionist underground groups) escalate. Abductions and attempted assassinations of British personnel were met by arrests and executions. On June 29, the British launched "Operation Agatha," a massive search for hidden weapons and Jewish resistance leaders and fighters. The Jewish community called it "the Black Sabbath."

Under curfew at the Afula hospital, my mother wrote to Kurt:

> *Curfew everywhere . . . complete day and night. . . . Chipusim [searches] in nearly all the Kibbucim [sic] . . . 2000—approx.— people arrested. 5 dead. Number of wounded unknown . . . the Jewish Agency . . . closed. Nearly all the members arrested. . . . No newspapers here for two days. We know nearly nothing of what is going on in the neighborhood.*

She had no idea when my father would get the letter; the curfew included a halt in mail service. In response to fragmentary news in Egyptian newspapers, my father sent her a political manifesto, outlining his despair about the possibility of either a political or military resolution and the uselessness of the great powers, which were preoccupied with greater world calamities.

My mother's last letter was a mix, reflecting both the surrounding horror and their personal joy: "My heart is bleeding for Yagur [a kibbutz near Haifa where the British found a huge weapons cache and arrested all the men]. . . . [Yet] it's so extraordinary that you'll come and stay, no more going away; no more rationed hours, no more buses to take you away. I can't say more. It's the bursting point . . ." She reminds him to keep and bring her letters, "I am playing with the idea to publish them (in a score of years). . . . *Nouvelle, Nouvelle Heloise en les lettres des deux amantes* . . ."[14]

* * *

After my father arrived in Palestine and my parents made the rounds

---

14. Referring to the twelfth-century letters of Heloise and Abelard. That, in part, is what I have done here.

My parents in Kfar Ruppin in 1946.

of relatives—the Arnsteins, now in Jerusalem and my father's father in Tel Aviv—they settled in Kfar Ruppin (without a fan). They worked wherever needed, then gradually found their niches, my mother first as a nurse and then as a *metapelet*—children's caretaker—and my father in the fields and carpentry shop, and, later, as a physics teacher in the regional high school.

In hindsight, in her memoir in 2015, my mother confesses: "The place looked horrid to me. There was malaria and mosquitos, no water, no electricity. When it rained we were in mud up to our knees. It was awful!" But she persevered, telling herself, "This is what I came for: to 'make the desert bloom.'"

My father also struggled with the inhospitable land and oppressive conditions, but he barreled through the hardships, armed with romanticism and idealism. In a short story written in 1946 he describes in florid, masculine language (deeply influenced by Hemingway) the hostile, yet alluring landscape and the passion of working its soil:

It was a strange place, repulsive at first and strongly drawing you later, in its torn wilderness, in its unruly, whim-ish changes, spots of deep, rich green sprouting isolated from what seemed to be a desert. The earth, which yesterday, turned up with [a] turiyah [a large hoe], was richly black, crumbled into the notorious whitish powder, looking barren and poor.

[But] . . . with water and cared for, this earth produced wonders, and there was plenty of water everywhere, as if . . . a joke in such a hot, dried-up place. From everywhere small streams, rivulets, springs brought their contribution to the reptile-like winding Jordan . . . The land waited for its dreamy prince—to respond passionately to his wet kisses. The land was a fierce, strange woman who will yield to a strong and merciless hand only; which, when ploughed, overturned, cut through by countless aqueducts and furrows, tortured and beaten, gave away its mysterious secrets, its abundant riches.

A man could become drunk with the morning air, the wholly [sic] stillness reigning around, the faint splash of the distant river.

In the early days my father was, at times, "drunk" with working the land and the community's engulfing closeness. But soon his more characteristic skepticism and pessimism colored his view, especially of the utopia they fervently believed they were building. Writing "Small Notes—before I forget them," he describes it as "a life, which sometimes appeared to be one of a tightly-packed human herd. . . ." Inevitably the kibbutz was riven with rivalries and power struggles, which he portrays in his 1946 essay, "A Strange Place":

You are under constant and often malicious control, all you say and do is registered and remembered . . . [by] the very people you are willy-nilly compelled to live, bathe, work, eat and decide important issues of life with . . . struggling against the most commonplace daily trivialities as if they were the most important issues.

My mother did not commit her thoughts to paper, but from early on began to stand out. She always had an original take on things, usually against the grain of the often-crushing community consensus. Sometimes she paid a high price. When my oldest brother, Gil, got sick as a newborn, she took him out of the baby nursery, where all infants spent day and night, to care for him at home. She was formally reprimanded at the *asefah* (the kibbutz weekly general meeting)—an unprecedented censure. When she brought him back, she earned more scorn by hanging a homemade mobile of colorful plastic saucers over his crib. Scandalous! The prevailing ethos set by the infant caretaker, who was herself childless but had received training, was that babies required a pure white, sterile environment.

Gil did not seem to suffer from this early exposure to color, nor from the trying circumstances of his birth. He had arrived in early February 1948, a period of frequent Jewish-Arab skirmishes.[15] The road to the Afula hospital was narrow, potholed, and favored by snipers. Two weeks before her due date, my mother went to Merhaviah, near the hospital, staying with a kibbutz member's aunt. She waited, alone and scared.

The night Gil was born my father happened to be on guard duty. He saw flashes of light from the neighboring kibbutz—a message in Morse code. He sent his partner, Gad, up the water tank, to decipher the message and respond with the kibbutz's spotlight. Gad scrambled up the iron ladder, took down the message and signaled back that it was received.

"So, what did they say?" my father asked when Gad came down.

"Nonsense, just making sure we're awake and paying attention."

"What nonsense exactly?"

"Merhaviah gave birth to a son."

"That's no nonsense!" my father called out. "That's MY son!"

---

15. Leading up to Israel's Declaration of Independence on May 15 and the "War of Independence"—the Palestinian "Nakba."

The Kfar Ruppin water tower. Courtesy of Kibbutz Kfar Ruppin's archive.

Seventeen months later, but in a different world—after the war had ended and the State of Israel was a firm reality—my brother Eran was born. This time there was no need to wait in Merhaviah or use Morse code, but how my mother managed a toddler and a newborn in the summer heat of Kfar Ruppin is unfathomable. Perhaps what made it bearable was the small fan the kibbutz by now provided and the improvised "desert cooler" my father had built. It was a wooden frame with sawdust packed between two mesh screens. It lowered the temperature by two or three degrees, a huge difference! Everyone wanted one and my father's career as a custom-order carpenter began. After he'd built coolers for everyone, expectations rose; people wanted tables, chairs, and bookshelves. It worked as a labor exchange: the "customers" took my father's rotations in the dining room or at guard duty and he put the same number of hours into fabricating their orders.

I was born on August 13, 1952. On my first birthday my mother wrote:

Me at two months old, with my mother.

It's your first birthday today, my tiny daughter. I am starting your diary a little late, but still not too late to remember the great events of your first year. . . .

The first months of your life were very trying . . . for both of us. The heat was dreadful, there were many days of 45°C and we sweated in the Baby Nursery. . . . I was covered with heat rash and you had boils on your tiny head, which certainly were painful to you, and even more to me.

Needless to say, I don't remember the heat or boils.

My very first memory is of climbing a jungle gym at the toddler house play yard. I still recall the feeling of great confidence as I climbed the evenly spaced rungs, and the trembling of fear and strain as I touched but couldn't grasp the first horizontal bar. Had I succeeded in grabbing it, I would have hung there, thrice my height above the ground, with no way back to safety. I have no recollection of an adult either supervising or coming to my rescue.

Many of my childhood memories have this in common: we children, climbing, running, negotiating with each other, completely on our own. As an adult I'm petrified—in hindsight. As a child, what I remember mostly is feeling free and bold.

Baby cribs with mosquito netting set up outdoors. Courtesy of
Kibbutz Kfar Ruppin's archive.

Left to right, my brother Gil, me, and my brother
Eran in 1953, on the steps leading up to the
hill (Ha-Giv'ah) where the kibbutz was
initially built.

My
Kibbutz
Childhood

We were minus 238 meters! But for Kibbutz Ein Gedi on the shore of the Dead Sea (at 423 meters below sea level), we were the lowest kibbutz on Earth. We were so proud! And it didn't come easy. As the bus wound its way from Afula, the central bus depot for the Jezreel Valley and all points north, and we passed the road sign declaring "Sea Level" with two lines of stylized waves below the words, every meter we descended added a bit of weight on our shoulders. One would think that air weighs nothing, but a column 238 meters high weighs something. . . . The air at Kfar Ruppin always felt heavier than it did in other places. It seemed to take just a bit more work to breathe it in. Old people on the kibbutz seemed just a bit more hunched over than they were anywhere else, and the tops of bayonet-like cypress trees appeared to be a tad lower than in other places. But we kids held our heads high. When our class climbed Israel's highest peak, the 1,208-meter Mount Meron in the Galilee, we announced to the groups from other kibbutzim that we had climbed a total of 1,446 meters!

Between first and third grade I was rather worried about all this. I already understood what it meant to be below sea level, so I was afraid that after big storms the Mediterranean Sea would overspill its banks and sea water would fill the whole long valley from Haifa to Kfar Ruppin. We would be under water, just like we had been millions of years ago, as attested by fossils of sea anemones and snails that we found in the fields. "From when this area was the bottom of the sea," our teacher said while showing us the fossils during Nature Class, unaware I am sure, of the fear she struck in my heart.

What if the kibbutz was submerged? Would we all drown and eventually become fossils, too? No, I was sure the people would be rescued . . . somehow. We'd swim to the edge, and the fire department or the army would fish us out of the water. Thank God, I was already a decent swimmer by then; I could swim at least ten laps across the pool and float for at least an hour. But everything else—the houses, the fields, the graveyard, maybe even the animals we tended in the children's farm—they would be sunk underwater.

I got over it when our class went on an annual trip, covering the length of the two adjoining valleys—Jezreel and Zevulun—from our kibbutz to Haifa, much of it on foot. When we hiked over the hills that rise at Tivon, just two-thirds of the way between Haifa and us, I realized those hills were high enough to block the seawater if it ever flooded the beaches of Haifa. The water could not make it past those hills, comfortably secure at 130 meters above sea level.

My worries assuaged, I could focus on the business of growing up with a lighter heart. I let the feeling of being special at -238 spread, elevating not just all of us on the kibbutz—adults and kids—but me personally. I, a girl from Kfar Ruppin, was special. That's when I started working on *the film*. It was a pretend documentary about me, fashioned after some of the children's books I loved about young girls: *Heidi, Noriko-san the Girl from Japan* (in English it was titled *Eva visits Noriko-san*), and *Gilgi* (*Pippi Longstocking* in English). Since I was both the main subject, and the film crew and the cameras were invisible, I could document any moment in my daily routine. But I could focus best when I was by myself, weeding in the vegetable garden, the time during the summer between third and fourth grade when I brought the cows back from the pasture to the cowshed all on my own, when I walked from the children's house to my parents' room, my feet on the paved footpath but my head in the clouds.

The film ended abruptly the day after November 22, 1963. A few months after I had turned eleven, Kennedy yanked me out of my fantasy world and planted me firmly in reality. It was Shabbat—the news had taken overnight to reach us. I was walking to my parents' room in the mid-morning, hoping we would go on one of our family hikes, since the weather was nice. A family visiting the kibbutz—I did not know them—was heading towards me on the paved path. Their young boy—maybe eight or nine—came rushing up to me and yelled: "A big man in America! They shot him!"

I had no idea what he was talking about, but he was so distraught that I remember his face and his voice to this day. When I got to my parent's room I asked about "the big man in America" and they explained. I was startled and confused; I certainly did not know what to make of it, but I distinctly remembered the sensation that I was shrinking at break neck speed, receding into a tiny speck within a godforsaken spot, 238 meters below sea level, while a huge world unfurled itself in front of my eyes.

In my sixties now, having traveled through a decent chunk of this huge world, having learned much more about the Kennedy assassination, and having lived in JFK's country much longer than I had in my homeland, I find myself returning to the stories from -238 meters and documenting, in writing rather than film, moments from the life of the little girl I had been.

CHAPTER 1

Coveting

"I am smitten by your shoes," I whispered as I leaned towards the woman in the row in front of me. She turned her head and smiled.

"Thanks," she whispered back, "we'll talk outside, afterwards."

We had to sit through twenty more minutes as the crème de la crème of the hip fiction and poetry scene in Montreal droned on. I should have been hanging on their every word, but most of the time I scanned the room looking for something more exciting than my nails to occupy my attention.

There was a modest audience, most of them seated below me in the steeply tiered small theatre. It was safe to peruse. Fake crunchy curls, teased blond mops, woven shawls, raw silk, and linen jackets. But then that woman just in front of me stretched her right leg out from its perch on her left knee. I heard almost nothing after I saw those shoes. She seemed inattentive too, pointing her foot this way and that, tilting her head slightly as if to assess the shoe from a more flattering angle. Was she admiring her own shoes or giving me a show?

Outside, the reading thankfully over, we immediately found each other. She stuck out her right foot, then pivoted on her left in a quarter pirouette. I wanted to clap but held back. Those were some shoes, but I am no Imelda Marcos.

"The funny thing is," the woman began without introducing herself, "I sat in more or less the same seat two years ago, at a reading more or less like this one, and said the very same words to the woman in front of me! We were both taking this writers' workshop."

"Same shoes?" I asked.

"Not exactly, but similar. Same company."

"Which is?" I urged her on.

"Pikolinos. After I saw hers I bought mine."

"Ah, Pikolinos," I purred. "Of course! Italian."

"Actually, they're made in Spain. But you can get them on the web," she said.

I nodded.

"And the workshop? You were a participant?" I asked, suddenly embarrassed about this shoe-worship. "Was it good? Useful for you? Have you published yours?"

"One short story." She cut off my hanging question, but then added, "The workshop? It was pretty good. But not as good as the shoes."

I had some writing homework to do from earlier in the day and now, also a date with the Internet. I shared a quick laugh with her and said good-bye.

Back at my laptop, the Pikolinos proved to be beauties. I almost ordered a pair. They would wait for me when I got home in nine days. But I held back. Not because of the price—which was high—but because of Dalia's shoes. The first ones I fell for, my first love. My first time coveting . . . I still tasted the bitter edge.

Actually, it was more the buckles than the shoes. I was three and a half years old. Six of us children in my kibbutz class were in room two of the nursery school. We spent our first year as toddlers in room one. Once we turned two-and-a-half and had fallen into step with the group sessions on our little white enamel potties, we graduated to room two. We were now counted among the "big kids." Kindergarten, a year away, was already on our horizon.

It was during the morning free play that I went indoors while everyone was playing outside. I must have been looking for something, but I don't remember what. I squatted down, low to the floor (well, I was only three and a half, so I was pretty close to the floor already), and scanned the room. A silvery flash from under one of the narrow metal-frame beds caught my eye. I slithered under it. The cool tile floor greeted my belly.

It was hard to see in the dark shadow under the bed. I pushed myself all the way to the corner. There it was, the thing that had shone. I couldn't tell what it was, but clasped it in my hand and slid out in reverse. I looked this way and that. Good; no one was in the room. I opened my clenched fist. A burst of sparkling light, a cold imprint in my hand. I let my eyes slowly trace the elegant metal rectangle, its perfect proportions. I ran my fingertip along the bar bisecting the buckle mid-way and wiggled the slender tongue that would push through the hole in the leather strap. It was a thing of such beauty!

No one had buckles! We had shoestrings: dark brown or light brown. New laces were a cause for celebration. Later, in kindergarten, we would forever practice tying and untying them. The tips would fray so easily; our parents had to smooth and stiffen them with a bit of wax. The first time a shoelace broke they'd knot it back together; the second and third time as well. But finally the day would come when the laces were beyond repair and you would earn a new pair. You didn't have to wait until everyone else needed new laces. Such a rare nod towards individualism!

So how did this spectacular shiny buckle get here? However it did, it was mine now, a precious jewel for me alone. I slid it into my pocket and walked outside. My hands burrowed in my pockets so no one could tell how tightly my fist held the treasure. I stood near the kids waiting their turn on the swings, but I had no need for such mundane entertainment. I walked over to the sand box but stayed outside, not wanting even one grain of sand to slip into my pocket and sully the buckle's gleam.

Then I saw Dalia. She was sitting propped against the wall with her shoes off. It was too chilly that February morning to be barefoot.

"Dalia, the *metapelet* (the caretaker) will yell at you for taking your shoes off," I tried to warn her. But she didn't even look up at me.

"Dalia?" I came closer.

Now she raised her eyes towards me and I saw they glistened with tears.

"What's wrong?" I crouched down next to her.

"My buckle fell off. From my new shoes. I lost it!"

She was crying now.

"What buckle?" I tried to tamp down the terrible thought that began to lap against the shores of my awareness. Her buckle? Not mine? But . . . and how in the world did she come to have shoes with buckles? Why her, when no one else did?

But I knew why. It was her limp. One leg was shorter than the other. She needed special shoes.

"It's not her fault! She was born that way," the metapelet chastised us when she overheard us snickering. I had always felt sorry for Dalia. But not anymore.

"See?" she showed me the left shoe. "A buckle just like this one fell from here," she lifted the strap of the bereft right shoe.

"I'll never find it," she sniffled.

"I'll find it for you!" I called out, a touch too enthusiastically. "I am a good finder. Come with me. Let's look inside."

"Put the shoes on," I told her and pulled her indoors with me. My face felt hot and my hands were clammy. I couldn't think straight.

Then, in a flash, I knew what to do. I slithered under Dalia's bed and wiggled around below it, then pulled my right hand out of the pocket where it had been lodged all this time. I scooted back, feet first, then butt, and then cupped hands.

Me at age four:
"Happiness is a
sandbox and a
messy face."

"There!" I opened my fist triumphantly. "I found your buckle for you. It was right under your bed, in the far corner."

Dalia hesitated. I grabbed her hand and pushed the buckle into it.

"See! I found it for you!" I charged out of the room.

It was my dark secret for years to come. A double-edged sword, really. I couldn't shake the shame and guilt, the debut of those feelings in my little heart. But I was also so relieved that I had thought of an honorable way out. I was proud of myself: how clever of me to pretend to find the buckle for Dalia! She would have to be thankful to me. Neither she nor anyone else would ever know.

* * *

Years later, both of us adults and no longer living on the kibbutz, I saw Dalia when she came to visit her parents. They lived next door to mine, so we stopped and chatted on the path, right at the point where it split, the left fork to her parents' and the right one to mine. We got caught up on kids, husbands, work, and travel.

"You lost a lot of weight," I said, taking a risk, admittedly a small one among women.

"Thanks," she smiled, "I still need to lose some more." She had been a chubby girl all our growing up years, an insult added to the injury of her limp.

"No, you don't," I protested and took a step back, pretending to gauge her figure from a good angle. "You look great. And nice shoes, too!" I added for good measure.

"Snazzy buckles, ha?" Dalia said.

"Yes, silver! Very pretty," I agreed.

"Yes, they are. Shiny . . . just like the one you stole from me. Remember?"

CHAPTER 2

Clean Sheets

"Wake up! Wake up!"

My blanket yanked off my face, I opened my eyes. In the fresh light of dawn I saw Roni and Dalia pressed up against my bed.

"Why? What?"

"It happened again," Roni whispered.

"It happened again?" I repeated as I came around to full awareness.

"You know, to Sammi," Dalia said.

We never said the actual words. I got up and quickly smoothed down my blanket.

"Let's go," I said.

We turned toward the far corner of the room where Sammi was perched on the edge of his bed, hunched under his blanket. He was pulling in the ends of the blanket under his chin so tightly you saw only his eyes and half his nose. We were certainly efficient for four-year-olds. We had had plenty of practice. This happened at least once a week. Sammi was the last one in our class of eleven—five girls and six boys—who still had this problem. No one ever talked about it. Not the three of us who shared his room, nor the kids from other rooms who occasionally woke up early and saw us in action. Not the grown-ups either, neither the metapelet nor anyone's parents. Did they even know? Did Sammi's parents know? Was there a conspiracy of silence or mere ignorance?

I rushed to the anteroom leading to the showers, where clean laundry was kept in two rows of triple cubbies. The lower row was for bottom sheets, slipcovers for blankets, and pajamas. I grabbed one of each. The second tier had one compartment for underwear, one for shirts and one for pants. I didn't need those now. I carried my bundle back to the room.

I knew Roni and Dalia had already stripped Sammi's bed by the smell in the doorway. Slightly pungent, with a chemical quality I did not know the name for yet. Though it wasn't terribly strong, I experienced it as overpowering, not in my nose, but in my heart. Shame—on Sammi's behalf—as if it were an entity standing on its own, right there in the middle room.

I put my bundle on the floor and, without a word, took the blanket from Sammi's hands. Roni held on to the edges of the blanket while Dalia and I tugged on the opposite corners of the slipcover. It was a hard job under normal circumstances, but with the large damp spot in the middle, it took all our strength. It was as if the wet patch didn't want to part from the cozy warmth of the blanket.

Meanwhile Sammi stood to the side, shivering in his wet pajamas. I handed him the clean pair.

"Quick," I said, "and put the wet pajamas on top of the wet sheets," I said as I turned back to help Roni and Dalia drag the recalcitrant blanket out. Finally the blanket released the cover, and Dalia and I set to maneuvering it into the fresh one. Roni rolled the wet bedding and pajamas into a tight wad.

"Push it to the very bottom of the dirty laundry bin," I said as he dragged the wet roll along the floor by its only dry corner, heading towards the shower room.

"I know!" he said.

"And make sure there is enough laundry on top of it so you can't smell it." I couldn't help acting as if I were in charge.

"I know that, too," Roni said. "I've done it enough times." He rounded the doorpost with the laundry.

"We better hurry," I said to Dalia as we lay down the clean bottom sheet over the thin mattress, smoothing it across the middle.

"Yes," she said. "We better finish before the others wake up."

"Or the metapelet comes," I added.

Roni came back and helped us with the final tugs on the slipcover, until the blanket was all the way in and we managed to do the buttons that closed its open mouth. Sammi lay down on his bed and we covered him up. He was still shivering, so I tucked the blanket around him.

"Pretend you are asleep," Roni instructed everyone, as we slipped into our own beds and pulled the covers up to our chins. A moment later we all heard the footsteps of the metapelet approaching the front door.

* * *

Years later, when Sammi was drafted, joining a highly selective combat unit, I saw him after the first week of basic training.

"How is it going? How are you holding up?" I asked.

"Good. It's not as hard as I was led to believe. The discipline, the endless push-ups, you know."

"Great!"

"The first night, though . . ." he stopped and his face got red.

"What?"

Sammi hesitated and stared at his feet, shaking his head. Then he took a big gulp of air.

"It came back. The first night on the base. I could have used you . . . and the others from our kindergarten room."

CHAPTER 3

Rice Pudding

"You'll stay right here in your chair until you eat it!" The kindergarten metapelet towered over me at the children's dining table. Unlike our regular caretaker, who was short, round, and jolly, she was broomstick thin, tall, and stern. Her elbows were so bony and her starch-ironed apron so spotless that I was definitely intimidated. But I huddled over my bowl, sucked in my upper lip and crossed my arms tightly on my chest.

"Hurry, now," she said.

I shook my head.

"Always so stubborn," she muttered to herself, then raised her voice: "The others want to go home already. It's already five minutes after four. You, you are holding them up."

Out of the corner of my eye I took a peek at my ten classmates already lined up by the door, ready to go to their parents' homes for the afternoon and evening. I could see my friends shaking their heads either in disbelief or in disapproval. Not of me, I was certain, but at this substitute metapelet, who didn't know our rule. I had told her the rule *three times,* but she dismissed me and said, "Just eat it!" The other children at my table, *all five of them,* had said I was right; each one of us was allowed one food that we did not have to eat.

Most of the kids chose spinach. It was always both runny and lumpy, and the brownish-green color was too close to what went down the toilet. It slithered down your throat in a revolting way. But I braved my way through it twice a week, at lunch, just to avoid rice pudding.

The funny thing is that rice pudding was a treat! Most of the kindergarteners loved it, served cold, a jiggling white blob slathered in berry syrup—ersatz, of course, just like our strawberry jam and plum sauce: sugar, gelatin, and a lot of red food coloring. The other kids cherished it. There were not a lot of sweets to be had except the fruit grown on the kibbutz: dates, pomegranates, and wild blackberries, which we picked in the wadis in 110 degrees, wearing long sleeves, long pants, and high-top shoes; otherwise you'd be scratched till you bled. Occasionally, the kibbutz purchased plums or apricots, overripe so bought at half price. Mostly the cooks in the kibbutz kitchen made them into compote.

I might have overcome my revulsion from the rice pudding had it been served with such stewed fruit, but that was never offered at our *aruchat arba,* the 4:00 p.m. snack meant to fortify us kids before we headed to our parents' rooms for family "afternoon tea." Israel was going through prolonged austerity, so our food repertoire was meager. We kids didn't mind that much. Only years later did I appreciate how my parents longed for real coffee, English tea, real fruit jams, and such. Once in a while we did get butter—small patties of surplus US army rations. Maybe there were other items too, such as canned corned beef or beans, but I don't remember those.

But I do remember the butter. First, because it tasted divine on thick bread slices served still warm from the bakery. Second, because of the stains on my pants. On occasion extra butter patties remained by the end of the day in kindergarten, and we were sent home with small squares of it wrapped in wax paper. I knew how much my parents would enjoy the butter so I ran home as fast as I could. But at one hundred degrees outside (which happened often), I never ran fast enough. A big circle of grease always bloomed on my pocket by the time I got home. All that was left inside my pocket was the wax paper.

Butter came once in a blue moon, but a big glop of rice pudding predictably appeared in the middle of our bowls once a week. I was the only one who didn't cheer. It was not just the distaste for it, it was also the treasured acknowledgment of uniqueness: that each one of us could pick whatever food they wished to declare, "I won't eat it!" I never wavered in eschewing rice pudding, even as the kids at my table smacked their lips. They may have been befuddled by my choice, but they respected it and perhaps even envied my will power.

"You must eat it." The metapelet raised her voice.

"I don't have to," I shot back.

She marched past the line of kids by the door and opened it wide.

"All right, children, you can all go to your parents' rooms now. Racheli will stay here until she finishes."

My friends filed through the open door one by one, the brave ones giving me a nod of support. The metapelet returned to my table and stood by the edge, tapping her foot. Tapping and tapping, arms crossed against her chest. I clenched my teeth and looked away from the bowl.

"All right," she softened, "you only need to eat two tablespoons." I clamped my lips and shook my head. It was not so much the rice pudding, pink syrup oozing down its sides. It was the injustice.

"Well then," she said, "I am leaving now, but *you will stay here* until you eat the whole bowl." She walked to the door and held it open for a few seconds, I guess to see if I would buckle. She went out, not quite slamming the door behind her, but giving it a very definitive bang.

I sat staring at the rice pudding, I suppose wishing it would evaporate or magically disappear. But I didn't even think of touching the spoon. Something totally new was happening to me. I didn't know the term *righteous indignation* then, but it felt hot and harsh but also sweet and exhilarating. It was a revelation: I, a child, was right. She, a grown-up, was wrong.

I have no idea how long I sat there. There was no wall clock anywhere and, anyway, I didn't know how to tell time yet. A couple of times I glanced out the windows, expecting it to be getting dark (which it wouldn't for another three hours). Then, the door of the kindergarten opened: my mother!

"Oh, you are here! What a relief!"

Years later she told me she had started to worry when I had not arrived at home by 4:30. I was a goody-two-shoes and always came straight home (even when not delivering butter). She had waited an extra fifteen minutes, in case I had found an injured gosling or gecko that had shed its tail (I often brought those home for her ministering; she was a nurse, after all). There was nothing to worry about really. The kibbutz was totally safe and all the kids over four years old walked home in the afternoon on their own. But recently I had been falling down a lot, bruising my knees on the edge of the concrete path, gashing my forehead on a branch protruding into the road (later on it turned out I needed glasses), so she went to look for me. The kindergarten itself was almost an afterthought, no more than the endpoint of the line retracing my path.

Now my mother saw the bowl of rice pudding and the way I was pressing my lips together in order not to cry.

She sat down next to me. "What happened here?"

"I won't . . ." a torrent of tears burst out. My mother took me in her arms and waited. Finally, catching my breath between whimpers and sniffles, I told her what the metapelet had said and done.

"It's not right!" I cried.

"It sure isn't!" my mother said. "Come with me."

She took my sweaty palm in one hand and picked up the bowl of rice pudding in the other. She marched us, me and the bowl, to the bathroom. With a dramatic flourish she dumped the rice pudding into the toilet. She let go of my hand and yanked the metal chain dangling from the water bowl that hung high above the *Niagara,* as we called that old-style toilet. Justice had prevailed, "rolling like great waters, righteousness like a mighty stream."

Years later, standing in the cold mist at the observation deck, I was floored by the real Niagara. But not quite as much as I had been by my mother's actions that day.

Top, mothers lined up at games for Shavu'ot. *Bottom*,
Here I am running into the arms of my
mother (*first on left*), after jumping over a
barrier made from buckets

CHAPTER 4

Sugar Cubes

Suddenly I got a grandfather. No one in my class had one. In fact, none of the kids I knew—both older and younger than me—had grandparents. One day when I was three, there he was—sitting in my parents' room when I arrived home from kindergarten in the afternoon.

"This is your grandfather," my mother said. "*Abba shel abba* (father's father)."

We were brought up to be straightforward and plainspoken, without much tutoring on manners. I didn't know whether I should offer my hand or politely bow, so I just smiled and blurted out: "I have a grandfather? Really?"

My parents shot him apologetic looks and fumbled among their words as they tried to excuse my ignorance.

"Come here," he said. "Have a look." He pulled his hand out of his pocket and presented me with a loosely held fist.

"What is it?" I asked as I came to his side.

"Open it," he said and gestured at his fist.

I hesitated. The skin of his hands was so pale, so thin. It made me think of the fragile membrane separating an egg's shell from the white. Peeling it off whenever we had hardboiled eggs for dinner always made me recoil with slight revulsion while it also fascinated me with its semi-translucence and stretchy flexibility. He smiled at me patiently and nodded toward his fist.

I gathered the bit of courage I had assembled in kindergarten by not freaking out when we spotted a mouse running along the walls, and peeled off his fingers one by one. The knuckles were a patchwork of fine lines, and his nails were shiny with beautiful white crescents at the tops. It would be thirty years before I'd learn that men, too, got manicures. His fists were easy to open.

Perched in the middle of his palm I uncovered two small, perfectly symmetrical white cubes. I didn't know what they were.

"What are they?" I asked. "Dice without dots?"

He chuckled and told me to pick one up and put it in my mouth. I gave my parents a puzzled glance. They nodded to go ahead. I picked up one cube between forefinger and thumb and slowly sailed it towards my lips. I was still suspicious. I wished my brothers were there so I could follow their example, but they were busy with the game of the season—soccer, marbles, cops and robbers—and they usually came home much later than me.

I opened my mouth and held my breath, placing the cube on my tongue. Immediately I smiled. Sugar! So sweet!

"The best thing ever!" I called once the sugar dissolved.

"You can have the other one, too," my now fully accepted grandfather said and raised his open palm towards me.

"Thank you," I said and picked it up as carefully as I had the first one. Then I handed it to my mother. "Save it for me for next week," I asked.

"There's no need," my grandfather said. "Next week you can have new ones. Every time you come to visit me in my room you can have one."

I looked at my mother for confirmation.

"Yes," she said. "Saba has his own room on the main path, the second room in from the cowsheds."

I knew exactly where it was and, if I gave up my usual shortcut, I would pass by there every day on my home from kindergarten. Not every day; I was afraid of depleting the sugar cube treasure too fast. And there were other treasures in his room, the most spectacular being an eight-volume encyclopedia of the natural world. There were books printed in Europe on such thin and sleek paper that turning the pages was like sliding silk between your fingers. And the illustrations! I had never seen a book with such vibrant color plates, such delicate, intricate zoological illustrations, reproductions of masterful etchings. I couldn't read it, of course—not only because I was just mastering the beginnings of the aleph-bet then, but because it was in German, and in Gothic script at that. But that didn't matter. I pored over the illustrations page by page, always marking where I had gotten to. When I finished the eighth volume after months of "reading," I went back to the beginning.

Once I even invited my whole kindergarten class to visit my grandpa after we had returned from a morning outing to see the cows and the tractors. First, I showed off the books, but I wouldn't let anyone touch them. Everyone had to crowd around me as I turned the pages, from one color plate to the next. To my delight, my grandfather had enough sugar cubes to give each child one. They talked about it for a whole week thereafter and my status rose several notches. I warned the kids that they could only visit MY grandpa if I invited them to accompany me. I don't remember that I ever did.

It was late the following spring when my grandpa went to the hospital. Shortly thereafter my parents sat all three of us down and told us that Grandpa had died.

"The funeral was this afternoon," my mother added to make it clear it had really happened.

"This afternoon? When I was at kindergarten?"

"Yes."

"You mean maybe I was taking my nap when it happened? But—"

"I know," my mother said in a tone that told me she was not pleased with the situation. Years later I learned that in those days it was considered self-evident that children should not go to funerals. She didn't agree with this "wisdom," but it was one fight with the kibbutz norms that she chose not to take on. So to me, my grandfather just seemed to vanish.

"What about the sugar cubes?" I asked sheepishly. I knew I shouldn't and blushed. "And the beautiful books?"

"We will bring everything here—whatever we want to keep."

The next day we went to his room and sorted through everything. I didn't realize how many drawings and paintings he had left behind. He became an amateur artist in old age and was really quite talented. Not that I realized it then. I am writing this looking at a pastel that hangs in my house of a spotlight on a whitewashed building on the Giv'ah—the hill in the middle of the kibbutz. The building and bushes around it are a faithful rendition, but the sky is right out of Europe: ominous clouds in many shades of gray, pierced by the last rays of light before the thunderclap—nothing like the sky at the kibbutz, which was usually a clean, flat blue.

My mother opened the box of sugar cubes, two-thirds filled. I counted them slowly: there were thirty-two left.

"If we divide them equally between you three kids, you'll each get ten and two will be left."

"Imma and Abba can have those two!" my older brother suggested.

"I could eat my ten cubes in two gulps!" my middle brother said.

"I'll eat one every other day and stretch them for . . . let's see," my oldest brother countered and frowned a little as he did the math in his head, "almost three weeks."

"No!" I said with great certainty, as if I were the eldest. "We'll save them and every year on the day grandpa died we'll eat just one. We'll take turns year after year. That way we'll remember him until we are grown-ups."

To my amazement, both my brothers immediately agreed. It was many years—the sugar cubes long forgotten—before, as an adult, I first encountered the traditional Jewish practice of lighting a Yahrzeit candle on the anniversary of a person's death.

CHAPTER 5

Kindergarten Antics

"Good night, children. Behave!" the metapelet called out and shut the kindergarten door behind her.

We all waited the requisite two minutes, counting thirty-two breaths. We knew we had plenty of time. Our parents put us to bed at 8:00 p.m., and after a short story or song they all left. The metapelet then passed by each room to make sure everyone was tucked in and quiet. She wished us good dreams and left. A kibbutz member would come between 9:30 and 10:00 p.m. and sleep on a cot in the main hall. Every member had to do it by a rotation that placed him or her on duty every three months, in the kindergarten, the baby house, toddlers' nursery, or one of the other children's houses with kids under eight.

We were only four years old, so we didn't know how to tell time yet, but we had figured out that once the two hands on the big clock in the kitchen made a single horizontal line, it was time to wind our games down and head to bed. I would always remind Sammi, in a hushed voice, to go to the bathroom before getting in bed. I thought it helped, at least some of the time, with the bed-wetting problem.

"Now," Roni yelled, and we all threw our blankets off and scooted to the middle of the room, as did the kids in each of the other three bedrooms in the kindergarten.

"Tug-of-war!" Arik called out at the top of his voice. He always called for that since it was his best event. He was taller by nearly a full head than the rest of us, and broader by about as much. Several kids shushed him. We had a system, after all. Each room held a huddle for a few minutes to come up with the best idea for that night's shenanigans. Then we would meet in the dress-up play area in the central room and vote for the best proposal.

We were only four years old but, growing up on the kibbutz, we had already been trained in group decision-making and democratic rules. Each room selected a representative for the night according to a rotation, so that everyone would have an equal chance to be a spokesperson. Then we voted. We kept track of who won each vote, and if we noted one room getting too big a share of the votes we kept it out of the running for a few days, until the score evened out.

We came up with everything you'd imagine and more. From hide-and-seek with all the lights off, to three-legged races and ghost stories. Arik wasn't the only one who liked tug-of-war above all; most of the boys did. But they agreed to vary things enough so that we girls would go along. Arik always pouted and often even cried. But we were used to it: for reasons we didn't understand at the time, his threshold for frustration was much lower than everyone else's. We got very adept at appeasing him. No one wanted to see him throw a tantrum or, worse—given his size—get aggressive.

My favorite activity ever was the flint stones experiment. For three nights in a row we tried to make a fire, as illustrated in a book we had in our kindergarten library about cavemen. In each room we huddled under a blanket and smashed the flint stones together. Fortunately for us, the kindergarten building, and the kibbutz, although perhaps not for our scientific education, we managed to generate lots of sparks, but none ignited the bits of toilet paper we had at the ready.

We were not as lucky with our next event: the long jump. It started as a simple long jump competition, from the windowsill at the back wall, landing as far as you could in the middle of the room. Soon we improved on it. We put a blanket on the floor, right where you landed; the combined velocity of the jump and slickness of the tile floor allowed you to slide atop the blanket another four or five feet forward. With practice, we had perfected it so that the most athletic and daring among us could actually slide clear out the room's door and into the hallway.

I mostly focused on not hitting my butt on the edge of the bed as I came flying down from the windowsill. I never made it all the way to the doorway. I went among the first in the night's competition and was relieved to simply land safely. Sammi, who was our room's champion, sailed through the doorway and landed five tiles—a full meter—past the door. Dorit from the room next door followed, but she reached only three tiles past. Next came Rafi from the last room down the hallway, landing halfway between Sammi's record and Dorit's spot. Our room was in the lead!

Arik was the last one to go. I wondered if greater weight and height were an advantage or a handicap. He climbed up to the window and crouched. "One, two, three!" everyone counted out loud together. But he didn't budge.

"Count again," he said.

We did. He still didn't jump.

"Fold the blanket double."

"That's not fair," Sammi protested. "You should have it exactly as the rest of us did."

"It's fine," Roni said. "He can choose how he wants the blanket folded."

"But—" Sammi began.

"It's not in the rules." Roni cut him off, speaking with authority, as if there were actually rules written down somewhere. "Besides, he is much bigger; he'll hit the floor harder. So he needs more padding."

Roni stepped into the middle of the room and folded the blanket.

"Not like that," Arik said. "Turn it the other way."

Roni frowned but pivoted the blanket around. I looked at Arik: his knuckles were white from gripping the edge of the window. His jaw was tight. I could tell he was clenching his teeth. Suddenly I realized he was scared. Should I help him get out of it somehow? He would never admit to being afraid. Did I want to help him wiggle out of it and save face, thus spoiling the fun of the competition? It would be to our room's advantage, handing Sammi and us a victory. But it would be an undeserved one.

I looked at Arik's face and knew he was terrified. Now I knew I had to help him.

"A grown-up is coming," I called out.

But before anyone heard me and turned to scurry back to bed, Arik jumped. He landed square in the middle of the folded blanket and flew forward, faster than anyone ever had. He stretched his feet out, apparently not perfectly straight. He went into a swift swerve, crashing into the doorpost: first his shoulder, then his side, and now his head flew forward and slammed into the doorframe.

Arik crumpled and fell sideways. We froze, then rushed to him: "Arik! Are you okay?" He didn't answer.

"He is dead!" Roni screamed.

"No! No!" everyone shouted back.

I knelt by Arik's side and took his hand. It was cold and sweaty. "Arik," I called, then shouted into his ear. Everyone held their breath. It seemed like forever.

Finally he opened his eyes. He blinked again and again, but didn't speak.

"Arik, look at me!" I brought my face close up to his. "Are you all right? Just nod if you understand."

He stared at me with vacant eyes for a moment, then nodded, very, very slowly. We breathed again.

"Can you get up?" Roni asked and slid his hand under Arik's arm.

"It . . . h-h-hurts," Arik blurted out.

"All right, just stay on the blanket," Roni said and turned to the rest of us: "Two kids grab each corner and we'll slide him back to his bed."

We scrambled to take hold of the corners and coordinate our slow steps as we pulled Arik, as if on a sled, down the hall, all the way to the foot of his bed. With all our strength we managed to lift him onto his bed, some of us pulling on the blanket, others pushing on his bottom. I ran to the kitchen and brought back ice in a small bowl. We took the socks tucked in everyone's shoes for the morning, which lined up neatly at the foot of each bed, and filled them with ice cubes. We placed them on every part of Arik's body that had been bashed in.

We quieted down as Arik groaned. Now we heard it: footsteps approaching the kindergarten. "Shall I tell the grown-up?" I asked Arik. He shook his head. So did everyone else. We scattered, running to our beds and hiding under the covers. By the time the kibbutz member on duty that night opened the door and stepped in, the kindergarten was under a blanket of silence.

I kept myself awake listening to the man's breathing. When I heard his snores echo in the hallway, like a tractor driving over loose gravel, I tiptoed to Arik's bedside. He was fast asleep. I wondered if I should wake him. I had had a concussion myself over a year earlier (caused, ironically, by Arik chasing me through the yard of the toddlers' house), and I remembered my parents waking me several times during the first two nights to make sure I was all right. I nudged Arik and whispered in his ear. He opened his eyes. "Are you alright?" I whispered. He looked at me—not comprehending. I whispered the question again. He nodded. I crept back to my bed. Twice more in the course of the night I got up and roused one of the other kids in my room to come with me and check on Arik. Each time he grumbled when we woke him.

In the morning Arik's roommates instructed him to stay in bed and pretend to be sick. They told the metapelet he'd been up at night with a fever.

"Did you wake up the grown-up?" she asked.

"No," Dorit answered. "It wasn't so bad and we brought him water to drink."

The metapelet touched Arik's forehead and declared he had no temperature now, but should spend the day in bed. Thank goodness—he could nurse his bruises under his blanket and not give us away. He said his head hurt and she gave him aspirin. And that was that! We were not found out.

We never went back to the long jump. In fact, for quite a while our nighttime antics were much more sedate, limited to scary stories, joke telling, and farting marathons.

* * *

When we started first grade, Arik really struggled. He could not memorize the aleph-bet past the first five letters; he got all tangled up in the numbers above ten, and he couldn't learn to add beyond using the fingers of one hand. I worried. By the time we were in third grade he needed to go to a special school. My worries grew.

Finally, I screwed up my courage and asked my mother, who worked with the special needs kids on the kibbutz.

"C-C-Could it be from hitting his . . . his head like that?" I asked, after I had confessed our nighttime games.

"No, don't worry. It was known already when he was a toddler."

I burst into tears; the relief made my body limp. My mother put her hand on the crown of my head, perhaps stroking my hair, perhaps feeling for bumps.

"Still," she said, shaking her head, "what in the world were we thinking leaving you unsupervised every night?"

CHAPTER 6

The Red Shoes

The red shoes gleamed in the middle of the row of dark brown winter shoes. "Like a rose among the thorns," the line from the Song of Songs, pops into my head now, but I didn't know it then; I was only six years old. My whole class, waiting in tense yet sweet anticipation, was seated on the low bench in the shoemaker's shack. I am not calling it that for the alliterative effect. It really was a shack, one of the "Swedish huts," scattered throughout the kibbutz. They were wooden buildings, some single freestanding rooms and others three- or four-unit boxcar-like structures. They were popular in Israel in the early 1950s. They must have been prefabs of some sort— probably World War II surplus barracks.

It was hot and stuffy, as if pockets of summer's sizzling temperatures had been trapped inside, even though outside the breezes of late September already made the adults much less grumpy and volatile. But we didn't mind. We first graders were so excited about our new winter high-tops!

Menke, the shoemaker, worked his way down the sizes, so the biggest boys got their shoes first. Arik, Rafi, Asher, Sammi, and Roni were already admiring the dark sheen of their new shoes. I was second among the girls. I fixed my eyes on the row of shoes, trying to calculate if the red ones would fall on my turn. How a pair of red shoes got mixed in with the brown brood of identical high-tops, I couldn't fathom. None of us could, I am quite certain. But there they were, beaming at me, sending me a secret message: "We are waiting for you; we are yours."

The red shoes' allure was magnified by my image of the magic shoes in a favorite book of mine at the time, *Racheli, Amos and Ilana*, by the beloved poet Fania Bergstein (published in 1946). I was certain that the book was really about our group; after all we had a Racheli (me), an Amos (my first cousin), and an Ilana. And, just like us, they were kibbutz children, and getting new shoes was a big deal. In the opening story, Racheli receives new shoes (brown ones, however), which, after a big rainstorm, turn out to be magical. One shoe grows large enough for Racheli to sit in and sail away on the puddles to the ends of the earth.

I stared at the red shoes. I didn't know how to pray, and I did already know that I wasn't supposed to anyway. We didn't believe in God, angels, goblins, witches, tooth fairies, or anything of that sort. But at that moment I wished that I did. I closed my eyes for two seconds and silently asked a Shoe Fairy I had made up on the spot for those red beauties.

I opened my eyes. It was Shoshi's turn. Menke took down the red pair. I swallowed hard and looked away. I couldn't bear the suspense. Shoshi tugged and pulled, getting the shoes on with great effort. She tied the laces in loose knots. She stood up and took three steps.

"No!" the shoemaker said. "They are too small for you."

"Bb . . . bb . . . but, they feel fine. They are comfortable. Really!"

"Maybe right now," Menke said and leaned over her foot, "but you see here," he pressed down on the very front of the left shoe, "I can feel your toes. These shoes will be too tight in two or three months and they have to last you a whole year."

Shoshi dropped down on the bench with a thud. She couldn't

bring herself to take the shoes off. Menke had to kneel down, open the knots, unlace the shoes, and pull them off her feet. He handed her a brown pair, one size larger. She took them in her hand and held them out to the side, the way you would hold a dead rat by the tail.

I was next. The red shoes were mine! I slipped them on. "Like butter," I said as they slid over my ankle. I wiggled my toes. Yes! Plenty of room. Room to grow at least another centimeter. I grabbed the shoelaces—even they were red!—and threaded them through the top three holes. I gave each a good tug and made the knots with almost perfectly symmetrical loops.

I stood up and walked across the small room. Good thing I didn't know about fashion show runways. I walked straight ahead and after four steps turned around and headed back to the bench. I froze an instant before sitting down, as I realized my seat was right next to Dalia, the shoemaker's daughter. Our feet were the same size.

Of course! Her father could not give the red shoes to her. He could not appear to favor his own daughter. But . . . I couldn't stop the rush of thoughts: she had that awful limp, her father was a lowly shoe-maker while mine was a physics teacher, and there was that buckle in nursery school. I still felt its cold imprint on my palm.

I looked at her, seeking her eyes. She averted her gaze. Her cheeks reddened. Stepping forward, I lowered myself down to the bench slowly, grabbing the middle slat to steady myself.

"No," I pressed the words out in staccato. "Even though they fit. I don't want them.

I want brown ones, like everyone else."

"Are you sure?" Menke asked.

"Yes, I'm sure."

I peeked at Dalia out of the corner of my eye. Her face was glow-ing. I bent over to take the red shoes off, pressing my face into my thighs and shutting my eyelids tight to push back the tears. I couldn't open the knot.

"Can I help you?" Menke asked.

"No! I can do it," I said.

I could feel all the other kids' eyes boring holes into the back of my head, but I took my time undoing the knots, loosening the shoelaces and sliding the beloveds off my feet. I bit the inside of my cheeks and placed the shoes on the bench, right in the narrow space between Dalia and me.

Without a word, she put them on. She got up and took several steps. Her limp seemed to disappear. Menke went through the whole routine, pressing the front of the shoe to feel for her toes.

"Is it tight anywhere?" he asked her.

She shook her head "no."

"So they are comfortable? You like how they fit?"

She nodded "yes," but didn't say one word out loud. She sat back down on the bench, took the shoes off, and cradled them in her arms.

The rest of the girls hurried through their fittings, each one wedging her feet into the same brown shoes. Our metapelet appeared at the door. We all lined up with our shoes tucked under our arms and headed back to the children's house. Dalia was right in front of me in the line.

I stared at the back of her head, trying to keep the shoes that she hugged under her arm out of my field of vision. She held her head high. Her shoulders jutted back as she puffed up her chest. *She's walking with a proud stride*, I said to myself, *but she still has that limp.*

CHAPTER 7

Aleph-Bet

"You know not everyone in our class is like you," my first-grade teacher said after she'd pulled me aside when everyone filed out of the classroom for lunch. She was sitting at her desk, in front of the blackboard, and I was standing at its side. I had to lift my eyes high up to search for a clue on her face. Her freckled cheeks and dusty brown pupils gave me no hints.

"What do you mean?"

"Not everyone is having such an easy time learning how to read," she said and cleared her throat with a small cough. "Some of the children are struggling."

"But it's easy!"

"For you," the teacher said. "But, like I said, not for everyone."

I blushed and sucked in my lips. The room seemed stuffy, and she grew a few inches taller.

"I understand," I said and hung my head. "I will be more careful not to boast."

"That's nice," the teacher said, putting her hand on my shoulder, "and at least sometimes let someone else raise their hand first to answer a question."

I nodded silently. Feeling chastened, I didn't want to hazard saying anything else.

"But that's not what I wanted to talk to you about," she said as she shifted closer to me and lowered her voice.

"No?" I let out my breath in relief and shot up an inch.

"No. What I wanted to ask you is to do something special, something very important. But you have to keep it to yourself."

"What do you mean?"

"I don't want you to tell the other kids about it," the teacher said. "Can you promise that?"

"Of course," I said, eager to hear my special task.

"I want you to help Rafi. He is really falling behind in reading and writing."

"Rafi? But Rafi is smart!"

I would have expected her to mention Arik, another boy in the class who was behind in every subject. She agreed. Rafi was smart. Still, he was having a hard time. He just didn't seem to be able to memorize the aleph-bet and put the letters together into words.

"You have to understand," she said. "He can't get any help at home, from his parents."

"I know!" I said, thinking myself so clever. "Of course, they only came to the kibbutz two years ago. It's not their fault that they don't know how to read Hebrew yet."

I had already realized a while back that Rafi's parents were different from anyone else's. His mother was a tiny package of a woman. She came from Italy and could neither master Hebrew nor find her niche in the kibbutz work life. For months she was what we called a *pkak*—a "cork," inserted to plug any hole that appeared in the *sidur avodah*—the job assignments schedule. Every evening in a small room suffused with cigarette smoke, off the entrance to the kibbutz dining room, the *sadran avodah*—job scheduler—would fill out a gigantic piece of paper with every job on the kibbutz assigned to a given a member. Anyone with any stature would have their permanent job, with those working in the fields and cow barn at the top of the totem pole. Their names and jobs were written in ink. Entered in pencil, with repeated erasures and rewriting, were names of newcomers to the kibbutz, social misfits and schlemiels, who drifted from job to job, filling in wherever a "hole" was created by someone's illness or absence, or where demand increased during harvest or weeding season.

Finally, after bouncing from the laundry to the kitchen, to the toddlers' house and then the sewing workshop, Rafi's mother was given a permanent job: cooking the few salt-free hot lunches needed in the communal dining room. She worked quietly in a far corner of the huge, bustling kitchen, managing with a very limited vocabulary: "*ken, lo, ha-ochel mukhan*" ("yes, no, the food is ready"). Rafi's father was a bear of a man from Salonika, where he had worked in the port that is famous for its burly longshoremen. He drove a tractor, hauling heavy loads from one end of the kibbutz to the other, a stevedore without a sea. They were totally out of sync with the *Yekkes* and Czechs who dominated life in the kibbutz.

"So I have a great idea," I said, sparkling. "Why don't I make them a chart of the Hebrew alphabet and what each Hebrew letter corresponds to in their languages. My parents can help me make it; they know their alphabets. Then Rafi can memorize it with his parents." The teacher shook her head. She squirmed and coughed again. "They wouldn't be able to read it."

"The Hebrew letters?"

"No. Any letters."

I was dumbstruck. I swallowed back the words on the tip of my tongue. My parents often spoke about their stellar education in the gymnasium in Prague, especially about studying Latin and Greek. In addition to those languages, they read Czech, German, French, English, and, of course, Hebrew (the latter never with the same ease and fluency, since, as they said, "The letters go in the wrong direction.").

I had never met an actual, real person, who was what my parents called "an un-alphabet."

* * *

I started going to Rafi's parents' one-room apartment every afternoon.

"If anyone ever sees me come here and asks you or me about it, let's say that we are comparing stamp collections," I suggested on the first day.

"But I don't have a stamp collection," he said.

That, too, was unheard of. All the kids collected stamps. Some lucky ones, like me, had relatives abroad and, on rare occasions, got stamps from foreign countries.

"I'll bring you some tomorrow. Duplicates."

That settled, we began our first lesson. I suggested we do two letters every day. That way, in just two weeks he would know the whole alphabet.

Every afternoon when I came, Rafi's mother thanked me, capitalizing on the Hebrew she had mastered: "*Todah rabbah!*" At the end of the lesson she would address Rafi in a garbled Italian-Hebrew mishmash:

"Piccolino, give her two *sukariyot*," she said, handing him a small bowl with half a dozen lemon drops. These were different from the candy we got every Friday afternoon—four small balls for each child, two pink, two white. Those little balls—despite the different colors—were all plain sugar with food coloring, nothing like the delightful mix of sweet and sour of the lemon drops. Had she brought them from Italy? I wondered. And if so, how? I always took just one, worried that she couldn't get more when they ran out. I was relieved that our lessons ended before the lemon drops did.

Rafi was smart! In a few weeks he caught up to everyone else in our class. Our pact of secrecy turned into a lasting mutual loyalty. I defended Rafi when the boys made fun of him when he chose to play dress-up with the girls and act in our improvisational plays, instead of playing the boys' ball games and "cops and robbers." As the only boy in our acting troupe, Rafi was assured of getting the best male parts: the king, the prince, the knight, and the soldier. Occasionally, he'd play a thief or a murderer, less honorable but more fun.

Rafi stuck up for me when I insisted on playing on the soccer team. "She is a better player than most of you, and you know it!" he said to the boys. He clinched his argument by saying: "And if you don't let her play, it's only because you are afraid she'll embarrass you by scoring the winning goal."

As the years passed, we shed our childhood games. In fourth grade we abandoned the improvisational theatre, and, soon after I started developing breasts, I quit the soccer team. Rafi and I held our friendship from a distance, as the boys and girls drifted further and further apart.

But something remained between us, so I was not surprised when one evening in the middle of twelfth grade Rafi asked if we could talk. We slipped off at dusk to the side of the hill at the edge of the kibbutz and sat on the sloping grass facing the Jordan River. We both looked towards the darkening hills of the Gilead Mountains across the border. I knew Rafi would have an easier time talking if we didn't face each other directly.

"I . . . I want to ask your advice . . ." he started haltingly.

"My advice, really? About what?"

"Mmm . . ." he stopped.

"About the matriculation exams? Which ones you should take? Want me to help you study?" I rattled off the options, thinking I'd smooth over the awkward moment. I was very studious and imagined he might look up to me on that account. We could study together—a reprise of first grade.

"No, no," he said, shaking his head.

"No . . . so?"

"The army. I have to decide what unit to try for."

"I see."

He clammed up for a few minutes and I waited.

"You know I can't ask my parents' advice," Rafi said. "They don't understand these things."

"But your older brother? He has already served."

Six years older than Rafi, he was in the paratroopers and greatly admired on the kibbutz for fighting in Jerusalem in the Six Day War.

"Yes, he knows about the army. But I can't talk to him about my real question."

"But, surely he knows more about the different branches and units than I do," I said.

"It's not about the different units. I know all of that stuff."

"I see . . ." I said. This time I waited.

"It's about me. He won't understand . . . but you will. I think you will."

I did understand. I glanced at him sideways. I imagined his face had turned red, but the light was too dim to tell for sure. I pressed my lips together and remained silent, so he could say it.

"I am different," he finally blurted out, "different from the other boys."

"I know," I said softly. I wanted to touch his arm, but didn't dare. There was a long silence. I looked away, tried to breathe noiselessly. But he didn't say another word.

"I always was . . ." he finally whispered.

"I know," I said. "I always knew. It's fine with me. I was different than all the girls. Remember I was Danny for a whole year!"

"I remember," Rafi spoke a bit more easily now, "and you played soccer on the boys' team."

"I wasn't too bad," I said, chuckling.

"And there was that class picture," Rafi added. "Remember? In third grade where you sat in the girls' row with no undershirt on and showed off your boy's haircut."

"Yes, I was so proud of myself then. All the other girls wore undershirts."

"Right."

"Except Esti," I said. "But she was just copying me."

"She copied you a lot," Rafi said as if it were well known. I had never thought of it that way.

"But for you it wasn't like it was me," Rafi continued. "You grew out of it after a year."

"I guess so," I agreed, though not wholeheartedly.

"But I never did."

"I know, Rafi. I have known all along."

"Really?"

"Yes. I have a relative who's like that—some kind of cousin of my mother. He is a doctor, a big deal at the one of the health insurance companies. The chief medical director. So you . . . you can be a success."

"Maybe, later on," Rafi said, his voice dropped so low that I had to lean in closer. "But not in the army. It's not like that there."

"You're probably right. I understand: the fighting, the aggression. It's not for you."

"Exactly. I . . . can't. I can't do it," he said, barely squeezing the words out. "But, of course, I have to serve."

"Of course."

"So what do you suggest?"

"Let me think," I said.

"I could go for a non-combat unit. In supplies or transportation," he said when a minute had passed and I had offered no suggestions.

"A jobnik?" I said, unable to hide my derision.

"Is . . . that . . . so bad?" he stuttered.

"You are a kibbutznik. And your brother was in the paratroopers. Everyone expects you to volunteer for a combat unit."

"I know," he sighed and laced his fingers together tightly. "I know you are right."

We sat quietly. It had turned dark and we could no longer see the mountains in the distance.

"A medic!" I said, breaking the silence. "Become a medic. Then you can serve, and with great honor. And you'll be taking care of people, not trying to kill them."

"You are so right!" he exclaimed. "Of course, that's the solution. Why didn't I see it?"

* * *

I was very pleased with myself that day: for letting Rafi know I knew, for letting him know it was alright with me, and for giving him what I thought was a brilliant solution.

I am still pleased about the first two things, but not about the third. Rafi was killed on the Golan Heights in the Yom Kippur War, tending wounded comrades under fire.

CHAPTER 8

Tiny Feet

Until I was nearly nine I didn't know the Nazis were bad. I was confused because of Esther's tiny feet. I had noticed them the summer I turned five, when she came to the pool with her kids on a hot Shabbat morning. Soon after that I heard the story of Cinderella. Such dainty little feet, Cinderella had, that she could wear glass slippers and dance in them at the ball. Wouldn't they hurt? I wondered, remembering how my new shoes pressed on my feet before I broke them in, the painful blisters.

And they were no dainty slippers, those shoes. They were chunky, stiff leather brown high-tops. "Hopefully good for two winters," said the kibbutz shoemaker who fitted us with shoes every fall and sandals every spring. It was almost a chastisement: "Don't let your feet grow too fast. We can't afford to give you new shoes every year. These need to last for two."

I had no delicate slippers, only mounting worries. I had heard that as your brain grows, so grow your feet. Side by side they get bigger in concert with each other. If so, I was bound to have huge feet. I was certainly already the brainiest girl in my class. Will I end up having boats for shoes? Did that mean I would never dance with anyone, let alone a Prince Charming?

When I glanced at my mother's bare feet I knew it for sure: big. Much larger than most women's feet on the kibbutz, especially the few who actually wore shoes with heels on Friday evenings. Already in kindergarten we disdained these bourgeois shoes (not that we knew the word). They were for fancy-city-women, not for proper kibbutzniks. But we were thankful for them because they made a loud clickety-clack on the concrete path leading to the kindergarten. They gave us a much-appreciated warning when these women came to check on us, an hour after our official bedtime. We stopped our antics and slid under our sheets, pretending to be asleep.

Perhaps the rumor about the brain-foot growth alignment was false? What useful information could I glean from the Cinderella story? Well, in addition to tiny feet, she was obviously very pretty— another department where I found myself lacking. But, while Esther was pretty too, her husband was no more handsome than any of the other men on the kibbutz. So the equation tiny feet plus pretty face equals marrying Prince Charming wasn't so simple, after all. I was too embarrassed to ask my mother. Or did I already sense she was sensitive about her big feet?

Now, beauty aside, Cinderella seemed both dumb and meek. How else would you explain putting up with the cruel, ugly step-sisters and doing their bidding, or losing your slipper on the steps of the palace? Any sensible person would have taken those precious glass slippers off before running down the stairs. She could fall, the slippers would shatter, she'd cut her feet on the glass shards, miss her midnight deadline, and the whole thing would go up in smoke.

But this was not very helpful. I already understood that you couldn't subject a fairy tale to logical analysis. I could draw no useful conclusion from a make-believe story. Now Esther—she was real, she had tiny feet, and she was no dummy.

At the pool I kept stealing glances at her feet, sheathed in very thin pink rubber slippers, almost as tight as a second skin. As she swam the breaststroke along the wall of the pool, the pink slippers glided up to the surface of the water like miniature gondolas, then floated sideways and deep down in a Lilliputian ballet. Everyone else swam barefoot. In fact, we kids spent most of the summer barefoot everywhere we went as well, even on the burning hot dirt paths and sizzling cement walkways.

We actually made a kind of competitive sport out of running barefoot from the pool to the children's house, some 150 yards away. The unpaved road was layered with fine dust, deep enough for your feet to sink in and be fully covered. If you stood still, that is. But you wouldn't, because that dust got so hot by midday that you ran for your life. If, like me, you were not the fastest sprinter, the bottoms of your toes—those pea size pads that were soft and smooth at the start of summer and hardened callouses by its end—bled by the time you made it to the safety of the shade by the children's house. I was a slow runner. I had to be faster, but then again, the bleeding toes were a sort of badge of honor, so I had something to brag about. The grown-ups didn't approve. "Put your sandals on!" they ordered us when we left the pool. We did. But once the flimsy metal gate clanked shut behind us, we took them off and darted onto the dusty path.

The adults, more sensible, came and went to the pool in all manner of footwear, some in the heavy work shoes they wore in the fields, others in the brown leather two-strappers we called "biblical sandals," and some in the wooden single-band clogs they wore in the "olden days" of the communal shower. A few women, those we derided as "fancy ladies," wore thin-strap black or white sandals with shiny metal buckles and small heels. How decadent!

Yet, before these well-heeled ladies went in the water, they shed their shoes, sandals, or clogs. All the adults did, but not Esther. She never removed her pink slippers. I couldn't take my eyes off her elegant, dainty feet. She also never wore sandals, so no one had ever seen her bare feet and I only admired them sheathed in those slippers or in shoes.

"How does she have such tiny feet?" I screwed up my courage and asked our teacher, my voice surely tinged with envy.

"The Nazis did it to her."

"The Nazis? Who are they? How did they do it?"

I was trying to imagine what cunning process they had invented for shrinking feet.

"Don't ask. It's not a topic for children."

"Did they do it to Cinderella too?"

"Don't be stupid."

I knew enough to shut up. While we heard the terms "Nazis, Holocaust, camps" and "the war," often enough, we were shielded from any actual information about what they meant. But we knew they were taboo subjects, something we would learn about when we were older. I would have to find out somehow about the Nazis and small feet. Maybe they could do it for me, too. Then I could be brainy *and* dance with a prince.

* * *

The trial of Adolf Eichmann began the spring before I turned nine. The court proceedings were broadcast on the radio every day. We kids were not allowed to listen. Only high school students had permission. But information trickled down to us. I learned much more about what the Nazis did. I remember the most shattering image relayed in whispers: people crammed together, stark naked, in the gas chambers. I did not understand "gas chambers." No one explained that. But I could paint a horrifying picture to myself of women, naked from head to toe, pressed one into the other in a long, grotesque line. The humiliation of one woman's pelvis pressed against the next one's buttocks leapt across time and space and stung me with the ferocity of a thousand bees.

I pieced together what the Nazis did to Esther. A Hungarian Jew, she survived Auschwitz and was herded onto the death march as the Red Army neared the death camp in January 1945. The survivors stumbled westward on the snowy roads. Esther had no shoes. She made it through alive, but not her toes.

CHAPTER 9

The Hungarians

E sther was one of only four Hungarians on our kibbutz, founded
by German Jews—Yekkes—in 1938 and then populated more
fully by Czechs arriving during the course of the war. The Hungarians had all come after it ended. Each kept their story of escape
and survival to themselves, like a small match flame sheltered from
the wind in their tightly cupped hands. Esther's tiny feet, the blue
numbers on Zultan's arm, and Yitz's premature wrinkles gave opaque
testimony to the hell they had been through. But not Bencze, with his
smooth face and ruddy cheeks, shaded by a thick shock of hair he
flung across his forehead. He always seemed jolly. "The ones who
seem most normal are the ones most scarred," people on the kibbutz
said in hushed tones. "They put all their energy into covering it up,"
the Germans and Czechs who had managed to escape the clutches of
the Nazis said to each other, out of earshot of the handful of "real
survivors" who had arrived after the war.

In short order, Esther married Yitz, the best looking of the three
Hungarian men, leaving Zultan, whom everyone called Zulti, and

Bencze to keep each other company. As the years went by, they became a kind of couple: two lone bachelors on a kibbutz filled with couples desperate to repopulate the world with children, stand-ins for all they had lost. The two Hungarians became the heads of the bachelors' table in the dining room, holding forth at breakfast, lunch, and dinner about national politics, kibbutz controversies, and, most importantly, soccer.

The bachelor's table was two tables pushed together to seat eight, which made up the central row of tables in the dining room. On each side of the room were single tables for four. That made for a comfortably wide alley between the rows where the servers pushed two trollies, the first with the meal's hot dishes, the second with salads and bread baskets and, for breakfast and dinner, yogurt and hard-boiled eggs. The dining room was small enough so that, by the time the trollies got past the first few tables, those in the last one could tell by smell what was being served for the day's hot dish. The building was a very large wooden hut, another of the leftover World War II "Swedish Hut" prefabs. It accommodated about 120 diners at a time, so as the kibbutz grew, meals stretched over two shifts. On major holidays, extra tables were packed in so tightly that we managed to squeeze in over three hundred kibbutz members and their guests for the communal Passover Seder or Rosh Hashanah dinner. The building lasted three decades, and in its last years, in the early 1970s, steel cables held the sides tightly bound to each other, so that they wouldn't succumb to gravity.

The kibbutz dining room rule was that you had to fill each table sequentially. If there was still an open seat at any given table, you had to sit with whoever was already there, rather than start a new table. Some kibbutz members came in prearranged groups of four or eight, friends or co-workers, so they could all sit together. Often people lingered by the entry double doors, peaking in every few minutes and pretending to read the notices on the large bulletin board with great care. In fact, they were waiting for a table to fill when they didn't consider those already occupying it desirable company.

Thursdays, the main course at lunch was always goulash. The same scene repeated every week. When the serving cart rolled by the server announced: "Main dish: goulash and mashed potatoes. Vegetarian dish: eggplant."

"Let me smell it," Bencze demanded.

The server placed a hefty pile of mashed potatoes, steaming with a slightly chalky odor, on a plate with a splat, then crowned it with a ladleful of goulash. She stretched her arm to bring the plate close to Bencze's face. He sniffed loudly three times as everyone at the table got a whiff of the dense smell of overcooked meat, slightly singed at the edges. For empty stomachs it was really rather appetizing, but Bencze bent down the corners of his mouth in a disgusted frown.

"You call that goulash? Where's the paprika?"

"It's not the famous Hungarian goulash you always talk about, Bencze. It's Czech goulash."

"Czech goulash? There's no such thing," he snorted. "But you Czechs lord it over us here on everything."

"True," Zulti suddenly chimed in. "We, Hungarians, are an oppressed minority here."

"Oppressed, shmopressed," the server said impatiently. "Just tell me: goulash or eggplant?"

"Goulash," Bencze sighed. "Eggplant is even worse. But give me a big canister of paprika."

"Go get it yourself in the kitchen. Ask someone there if you can find your way through the boiling pots. I have a whole row waiting," the server said, pointing to the line of tables stretching to the end of the dining hall.

Bencze got up and headed to the kitchen after a loud declaration of the one response he had to nearly all topics: "Eh . . . They don't know what they are doing." As was often the case, Bencze's tablemates dismissed his comment, some with a wave of the hand, others rolling their eyes. But when the subject was more important, such as politics, kibbutz policies, or soccer, they matched him with "And *you* don't know what *you* are talking about."

Bencze got on his high horse when, at the end of the 1950s, Isra-el's fledgling national soccer team began to play internationally but was hopelessly inadequate against the European teams. "In Hungary they wouldn't make it out of the village's regional league," he announced. "Puskás could have dribbled past any one of them when he was eight years old."

"You and your Puskás . . ." one of the non-Hungarians bachelors at the table said with a dismissive fling of his hand.

"Puskás, of course! The greatest Hungarian soccer player ever!" Zulti, who actually had no interest in soccer, jumped in.

"Puskás is the only name known by those, like you, who don't know anything," Bencze said. "He is but one of the 'Magnificent Magyars.' The others are just as good: Kocsis and Bozsik, and in '38—you know they almost got the World Cup—there was Sárosi and Toldi and—"

"Do their names have to rhyme to get on the team?" the same fel-low said, still trying to puncture Bencze's bubble.

"Don't be an idiot!" Bencze replied. "There was Sas and Kohut and Zsengellér." He looked around at the faces ringing the table and shook his head: "Why am I wasting my time on you provincials?"

An avid soccer fan myself during this time, I lingered by the bach-elors' table during these conversations. No one noticed me; no one suspected a seven-year-old girl was eavesdropping on the men, trying to swallow Hungarian soccer stars' names as if they were plump, juicy grapes. All the other kids always made fun of the Hungarians, mostly of their accents in Hebrew, but also of the Hungarian excla-mations they would let slip out: *Istenem* (my God), *gyere ide* (come here) and *semmiképpen!* (no way).

We were all used to our parents' Czech with its strings of words with one vowel for every four or five consonants, crowned by a full sentence with none: *Str prst zkrk krk* (Stick your finger in your throat). And the tearing-your-hair-out-but-still-loving exhortations when we misbehaved: *Yeshishmaria Yozefa! Krootzinal!* And, because I was both a bit of a klutz and a tomboy, *Tczuniya prasse.* (It took years before I thought to decipher these: "Jesus, Mary and Joseph," "the crucified," and "dirty little pig."). But Hungarian had a totally different music to it—to my ear, intriguing, to everyone else's, ludicrous.

A few years earlier, in the summer of 1956, before I had any awareness of either soccer or politics, Hungary was making modest overtures towards moderation and democratization, and the kibbutz scraped together the money to send Bencze on a visit back home. Esther and Zulti did not want to go. "There is no one left," they each said. Bencze was not very specific about his reasons for wanting to go. All he said was: "The country is still there."

"But Bencze," one particularly combative member of the bachelors' table said, "like Zulti said, there's no one left. It's only *goyim*, blast their bones. Stole our houses. Not to mention aided the Nazis—"

"Don't say that!" Bencze shot back.

"But it's true!"

Bencze didn't answer. He got up without a word, picked up his plate, cutlery, and water glass and headed off to deposit them in the large tubs of steaming soapy water, to soak before those on dishwashing duty started scrubbing them. Those remaining at the table exchanged puzzled glances—Bencze was always the last one to get up from the table.

"What?" the combative bachelor asked. No one answered. Then Zulti shrugged and shepherded the conversation back to soccer.

It was very rare for any kibbutz member to travel abroad in those days, so when, after a month, Bencze returned, for weeks people asked him for stories. "What was it like, back there?" they asked over and over. "Back there, back there" seemed to pull them somewhere far away, perhaps to the Prague of their youth, even though he spoke of Hungary. Bencze talked about the still-beautiful forests, the still-tasty food, and the crumbling buildings—destruction wrought during the war and then by the Communists. He said nothing about people. No word about finding anyone. So no one pried.

By the end of the summer of Bencze's trip, the bachelors' table resumed its usual conversational fare. Hungary faded away except during the heated discussions of the previous Shabbat's soccer matches. Bencze returned to his motto: "They don't know what they are doing," and everyone else went back to disregarding his opinions.

The dramatic overthrow of Communism in Eastern Europe came well after the gradual, no-fanfare fading away of the ironclad collectivism of the kibbutz of my childhood. By now everyone had enough money in their personal accounts to shop in the cities for whatever they wanted, and to travel abroad, on their own dime, every few years. Most people began in Europe, but soon ventured farther—trekking in the Far East, going on African safaris, and driving across North America. But not Bencze. It seemed he never even traveled to Tel Aviv, let alone any of those more exotic locales. It was only Hungary, every summer. His stays grew longer and longer—three weeks, a month, eventually nearly the whole summer. The gossips in the kibbutz began to speculate that he had a woman back there. "A woman? Bencze?" Zulti dismissed them when they tried their theory on him, as the Hungarian expert. "What? Are you suggesting a man?" a particularly daring bachelor asked. "Ppfff," Zulti bristled. "Now all I can do is quote him: 'You don't know what you are talking about.'"

When, after his summer trip in 2010, Bencze's liver began to fail and he was hospitalized, his seat at the bachelors' table was left empty.

"Let's hope he comes back soon," everyone said. "Maybe there's hope."

"He's not coming back," Zulti said in a definitive tone, projecting across the table so everyone could hear.

"But there are all these new treatments . . ."

"You don't know what you are talking about," Zulti said, more softly now, and shook his head.

The conversation broke into near whispers between people sitting right next to each other. Many wondered about terminal liver disease in a man who had seemed so healthy. Jews, after all, did not suffer from alcoholism and were not prone to cirrhosis of the liver. Maybe he did drink? When he was there, in Hungary? What else was there for him to do there all summer? Slivovitz? Vodka? And why assume it was only in Hungary? The speculations swirled and swelled around the kibbutz. Zulti did not say anything, but his enigmatic smile suggested he knew more than all of them put together.

Esther went to the hospital in Afula twice a week and sat by Bencze's bedside from morning until afternoon, then headed back to the kibbutz on the 404, the 4:00 p.m. bus. Bencze was unable to eat, and an IV kept him hydrated. The day before Yom Kippur, Esther tried to joke with him, lift his darkened spirits just a tad:

"So, Bencze, finally you'll fast on Yom Kippur!"

Hardly anyone of the older generation on our once militantly secular kibbutz fasted. When I was a child, Yom Kippur was an ordinary workday. Sometime in the '70s, in a gesture towards new members who had come from more traditional families (and the militancy fading side by side with the collectivism), it was changed into a holiday. Not much in the way of observance, but no work either.

"Well," Bencze mustered up his strength, "That would be a first in my family!"

"Really?" Esther asked, "Even back in Hungary when you were a child? Your parents, or at least grandparents—nobody fasted?"

Bencze closed his eyes and let his breathing fill the silence for a long while. Finally he opened them and scooted up a little in his hospital bed.

"All these years, Esther . . . You didn't know? You didn't suspect?"

"What are you talking about, Bencze?"

"I am not . . . Jewish."

Esther opened her mouth to respond, but Bencze stopped her with his open palm.

"At the end of the war . . . I was eight, maybe nine, living on the streets in Budapest with a gang of older boys. We survived by stealing. Somehow in the course of the first years of the war my family disappeared. I don't know how. I was too young to remember."

He rested for a moment.

"Water," he whispered.

"Here." Esther brought the cup close to Bencze's face and slid the end of the bendable straw into his mouth. It seemed to take a great effort for him to suck up a teaspoonful of water. "Drink more," Esther urged, but Bencze shook his head. He spoke again:

"The guys from the Jewish Agency found me on the street one day."

"You mean the people who went all around Europe where the Nazis had been to find hidden children and rescue them? I heard stories about that," Esther said. "I had a baby brother but . . ." her voice trailed off.

"Yes," he nodded. "Those fellows. They found me right after a bigger boy had beaten me up and stolen the half-rotten apple I had filched from a peddler. I think they had seen me—us boys—before. They cleaned me up and gave me a square of chocolate."

"What's your name," the tall one among them who spoke good Hungarian asked, bending down, close up to my face.

"Bencze," I said.

"Listen, Bencze, listen good now! Before you get big enough to fight back, these boys will kill you. Why don't you go back to your parents?"

"Dead," I said.

"Grandparents? Uncles? Any family at all?"

"Nobody."

The agency man stood up and whispered to his friend for a minute, then bent back down towards me.

"Listen now—really carefully. We are organizing a group. Jewish boys who have been in hiding—we're going to Palestine, to a kibbutz. You don't know what it is, but they'll take care of you there. You'll have food, clothes, showers, a clean bed, everything. And you know, it's always sunny and warm there and oranges grow everywhere."

It sounded good. What other choice did I have?

"Let's see . . . Bencze . . . Just tell them your name is Benjamin."

"Ben-ja-min," I repeated.

"Good boy," he said. "A smart one," he told his friend. "And one more thing." He spoke more somberly now. "Never let them see your little pöcs down there. Always go to the bathroom and the shower by yourself. Later, when you see the doctor, show it to him. They'll take care of it."

So . . . after a few years in the Youth Aliyah School, I came to the kibbutz.

"I remember when you arrived," Esther said.

"Me, too. And after I shortened my name to Benja, and gradually let it slide back to Bencze. Nobody seemed to notice."

Bencze's head sank into the pillow, as if it suddenly weighed twice as much as before. Esther sat by the bed and, after a while, and for the first time in their lives, they held each other's hands.

Two days later Bencze was at the very end. Esther came to the hospital with the kibbutz nurse, for what she knew would be the last time. They sat by the bed. Bencze opened his eyes part way, the slits showing only slivers of his blue pupils. He tried to speak. His voice was so weak that Esther had to bend over him and put her ear within an inch of his lips.

"I know . . . what is happening," Bencze whispered.

"We are here," Esther whispered back.

"What"—Bencze pushed the words out with great effort—"What . . . do . . . you . . . do now?"

"What do we do?" Esther asked.

"You," Bencze repeated, "Jews."

"Ah." Esther understood. "We say the Shma Yisrael. We'll help you."

"Shma Yisrael," Esther and the nurse began to recite very slowly. Bencze's lips moved, but his voice could no longer be heard. With great effort he raised his right hand and touched his fingers to his forehead.

"*Adonai Eloheinu,*" they continued. Bencze's hand flitted down, landing for an instant in the middle of his chest.

"*Adonai.*" Bencze's fingers grazed his left shoulder.

"*Echad.*" Bencze let his hand come to a final rest on his right shoulder, where it stayed until he let out his last breath.

CHAPTER 10

Escape from the Children's House

"Let's all run out of the children's house and hide in the bushes," Sammi called out. "Then, when the substitute metapelet comes back and can't find us, it will be so funny! Good idea!" everyone cheered.

Our regular metapelet was sick. She would never have left us alone during the afternoon rest. She'd know we'd be up to no good if left unsupervised. But Rosa, her friend who covered for her, was naïve, assuming there was no harm in leaving eleven first graders, all tucked in their beds, for ten minutes while she went to the laundry to fetch our clean clothes.

"When she goes towards the soccer field to look for us we'll jump out of the bushes!" Esti said.

"No! We'll wait until she gets close to the bushes and jump out and yell 'Boo'!" Roni improved on Esti's idea.

Everyone agreed it was a splendid idea. Barefoot and without putting on any clothes beyond the underwear in which we supposedly slept during the afternoon siesta, we ran out of the children's house. We headed to the side of the building and into the bushes. We hadn't taken into account the thorns, so there were several yells of "ouch," and "ay," but we shushed them. We agreed it was all right to whisper amongst ourselves until we heard the rattle of the laundry cart's wheels as it approached the building.

We waited, talking and giggling.

"Sh, sh!" Sammi hissed and we fell into silence.

The metapelet wheeled the cart up to the front door and went inside. Now we could whisper again for a little while. It would take her a few minutes to put away the clean laundry in the cubbies near the bathrooms and go down the hallway peeking into our rooms to check on us.

Waiting made us notice the thorns again, and how dusty the dirt was where we'd sat down without forethought.

"The metapelet will not be happy about us getting our underwear dirty," I said in a low voice. "We might get in trouble for that."

"She'll forgive us," Sammi said. "She'll be laughing so hard about our trick."

"I hope so," I said.

Just then the door of the children's house flew open and a shriek like I'd never heard before rang in the air: "*Ye! Ye . . . Yeladim!*" The metapelet was standing in the doorway and holding onto the door-frame as if she were going to tumble down. She kept calling out, "Children! Children! Where are you?" in such a desperate way that we all looked at each other first with puzzlement, then with fear.

"What's wrong?" Roni whispered, "Why is she so upset?"

"We better come out," Dalia whispered too, but louder than Roni had.

"But she hasn't looked for us yet," Sammi said.

"She isn't going to, don't you see?" Dalia said. "Look at her!"

We all looked at the metapelet. She had sunk to her knees and was sobbing now. We couldn't believe it. We froze, not sure what to do. We certainly couldn't come near her when she was in this state.

Suddenly she jumped to her feet and started running towards the dining hall, screaming "Help! Help! The children are gone!" Before we could move, she was gone. Without a word, we came out of our hiding place and slunk back into the children's house. We dusted our bottoms as best we could and slid into our beds. We waited in total silence.

Soon, the metapelet came back with three other adults. One of them, the kibbutz nurse, was supporting her and talking to her, trying to calm her down. The other two women walked down each of the two hallways, standing at the doorway of each room and counting the heads on the pillows.

"All the children are here, in their beds," they each reported to the metapelet.

"But . . ." she choked on her words.

"Just wait here. Sit down. I'll get you some water. Then I'll find out what happened," one of the two women said. She came to my room and called me to come with her. She was my parents' neighbor; perhaps that's why she picked me. In the hallway she asked me to tell her the truth. I did. She shook her head, over and over.

"How could you do that?" she asked.

"But . . . it was just a prank. A silly ppp . . . p . . . prank."

"For you, maybe," she said, her eyes boring into me. "Not for her."

"But—"

"Not for her," she repeated, each word like a hammer blow. I knew not to ask why.

"You have no idea," she added and sent me back to my bed.

I had no idea. I knew we had done a horrible thing, but I didn't know what or why. Rosa left, still leaning on the nurse's arm. One of the other two women stayed with us until it was time to get up, get dressed, force the afternoon snack down our throats, and go home to our parents' rooms. No one said a word.

At home I tried to push it out of my mind, but my mother could tell I was struggling with something. "What happened?" she asked. I told her everything.

"I know we did a bad thing, but was it really that bad?"

"Not for you," my mother said, "but for her, for Rosa."

"Why?"

"I'll tell you when you are older. It has to do with the war."

I hung my head. Anything to do with "the war" was something terrible that we, children, didn't need to know about yet. That's all I could tell my classmates when I came back to the children's house that night. Others had been told something similar. No one knew more than that.

After the Eichmann trial, people's stories started to leak out. One kibbutz member after another, about whose past I had known nothing, turned out to have a hair-raising story. Rosa, too. She had been a young single woman in the Krakow Ghetto. She had no family responsibilities so she was drafted to be a teacher. She was in charge of twenty children ages four to six. She taught them their letters and numbers in a makeshift classroom. The room was dark and dank, so whenever the sun shone, she took the children for a walk outside. She always made sure to pass by the pharmacy.

"Say good morning to Pan Tadeusz," she would instruct the children. She thought it was important to show them that there was a gentile, at least one left in the world, who liked Jewish children. He would smile and wave to them and sometimes step into the ghetto street and give them lemon drops.

There was another gentile who liked Jewish children, the blond-haired, blue-eyed ones. Him, Rosa tried to avoid. The longing in his eyes when he looked at them, especially four-year-old Hannah, made Rosa's skin crawl. But as an SS officer, he had the run of the place and found ways to learn of the children's outings. At first, he just stood to the side and watched. But after a while he began to ask Rosa if he could hold Hannah in his arms, for just a minute. He was very polite, even a little timid, but Rosa knew she'd better agree.

And he was gentle with Hannah. Hannah didn't know better; she laughed when he tickled her and didn't seem to mind when he gave her a peck on the cheek before putting her down. Rosa swallowed hard but told herself it wouldn't hurt anyone. She never told Hannah's mother. She hoped no one else had either.

One afternoon the officer surprised her on her walk with the children at a narrow alley between two buildings. There was no one else in sight, neither SS men nor other Jews. He pulled a photograph out of the inside pocket of his starched coat. His brass insignia flashed as he pivoted towards her.

"Meine Frau," he said and thrust the photo under her face.

His wife had lustrous blond hair, which fell to her shoulder in soft waves. It was a black and white photograph, but Rosa was sure the wife's eyes were blue, just like Hannah's.

"Aber keine Kinder," he said in a hushed but urgent tone.

Rosa looked down and said nothing. She could hear the pleading in his voice. She nodded, but still kept her lips sealed tight. He stepped back and slid the photo inside his jacket.

"Keine Kinder! No children!" he started yelling. His eyes turned fierce and his mouth contorted. Rosa tried to sink her head between her shoulders and turned towards the children.

"March!" he barked and clasped his palm on the butt of his pistol.

"Let's go now, children." Rosa forced out a cheery voice and led her brood back to the classroom.

On the first day of the liquidation of the Krakow Ghetto, Rosa was ordered to march the children out of the classroom to the trucks. She led them down the street, past the pharmacy, where Tadeusz Pankiewicz stood watching. His face was contorted by a painful grimace.

"I am the witness," he whispered to Rosa as she passed by him.

The SS officer was waiting only a few yards away. He approached Rosa, looking left and right to make sure no one saw him.

"Give me the girl. I can save her," he said under his breath.

Rosa froze. Her eyes darted from side to side. She stiffened her arms. Bewildered, she didn't move and didn't answer.

"Give her to me," the SS officer demanded, louder now.

Rosa still couldn't move.

"All right," the officer said, "you, too."

"W . . . w . . . what?" she stammered as it dawned on her what he was saying. "But the other children . . . All the other children?"

Before she fully understood what was happening, the officer scooped up Hannah and dragged Rosa by her arm, pulling her inside the pharmacy.

Inside the darkened office, Rosa saw several people pressed against the walls. She recognized two women and one man from the ghetto, though she didn't know their names. There was no time to sort things out. The SS officer dropped her arm and, in a flash, was out the other door to the Aryan side, Hannah in his arms.

Rosa gasped and turned around to head back to the ghetto. She opened the door but Pan Tadeusz pushed her back in. He slid inside and shut the door.

"No!" he said to her.

"But the children!" Rosa called out.

"Sh . . . They are gone already."

"But, I must!"

"No," Tadeusz said again and grabbed her arm. "It's too late for them."

She stared at him. She opened her mouth to speak but no words came out.

"But we can save you," Tadeusz continued in a softer voice, "you and the others who managed to get in here."

Late that night, under cover of darkness, Tadeusz and his two female assistants escorted the six of them in pairs and handed them over to Polish underground fighters, who helped them escape from Krakow.

When she arrived at the kibbutz after the war, Rosa said she would work anywhere except in the children's houses. And that's how it had been for years: kitchen, cows, chicken coops, laundry, but never the children's houses. Except that one day when she had worked at ours, covering for her friend who had suddenly come down with a high fever.

CHAPTER 11

From Now On, Call Me Danny

"From now on my name is Danny," I announced to my third-grade classmates at lunch. "You should all call me that. Only that."

"Even in class?" Roni asked.

"Well . . ." I hesitated. "When the teacher calls on me I have no choice. But you all must only use only Danny—*all the time.*"

Everyone nodded in agreement. In our small class of eleven I usually got my way.

I had mulled over the name for a long time. What suited me most? It had to be a common name, a quintessential boy's name. Of course, not the same as any boy's in my class, or the grades right above or below us, since they shared many activities with us. I am not sure why Danny appealed to me above all other names. Could it be because it was actually ambiguous and could be a diminutive of Daniela, a fully legitimate girl's name? Perhaps I had prepared an honorable way out for myself in case "being a boy" backfired.

But, right now, I was determined, and pressed full steam ahead. Just changing my name was not enough, of course. I got a boy's hair-

My third-grade class. I am second from the left in
the seated row.

cut when the barber from Beit She'an, the nearby town, came for his
regular visit, the first Friday of the month. With a wet comb, he styled
a tall cowlick above my forehead. Cowlicks were all the rage and even
appeared as a marker of confident masculinity in a popular song
about Dudu, the heroic Palmach fighter. Generally, I wore tank top
undershirts in place of the short sleeve ones the girls were given, but
I sat proudly, bare chest puffed up, shirtless in a row of girls for the
annual class picture.

I am not sure if playing soccer begat wanting to be a boy or vice
versa. I did love the game and was pretty good at it. I played either
goalie or defensive center. Since I was not much of a runner, I left the
offense to the other boys. I also didn't want to humiliate the opposing
team's goalie. What if *a girl* scored the winning point?

My position on the team got a big boost when I received a T-shirt
from relatives in America. It was imprinted with an oval in the middle of the chest: two white pines on a dark green background and the
words "Pine Grove." No one—not one person on the whole kibbutz,
man, woman, or child—had a T-shirt with a picture on it, let alone

words in English. And the timing was perfect. Not long before, the kibbutz had decided that members could keep clothes they got as presents "from the city" as their private possessions. We no longer had to turn them over to the general clothing stock, to be rotated among all children in our class who wore the same size.

Nothing could stop me. I had a T-shirt that everyone coveted, played goalie on our soccer team, and sat bare-chested with the boys. And I allowed only my teachers and parents to still use my old name. My brothers, four and three years my seniors, never called me Racheli anyway—it was always one nickname or another, mostly "ha-tzola'at," the lame-footed one. But for the rest of the world, I was Danny!

My parents made no big deal of my conversion, likely believing it would soon pass of its own accord. But it persisted, through the third grade, the following summer, and into the beginning of the next school year. I wonder if my parents did begin to worry.

At the start of fourth grade our metapelet announced that from now on the boys and girls would shower separately, and the children's house would be divided between a boys' wing on one side and a girls' corridor on the other. I demanded a discussion, a vote by us kids. I believed I could sway my whole class against it. Sure, separate boys' and girls' showers and bedrooms had to come at some point before we hit puberty, but why so soon? I was sure I'd convince my class-mates by referring to the "abominable behavior" we had heard about in the grades above us.

It was an old story. Seemingly every class went through a period—often several years—of "peeking and counter-peeking." The boys always started it, but once the girls found out, they retaliated. It was pretty clever, I had to admit. They attached a small hand mirror to a stick shoved partway through the narrow drainage canal that ran through both shower rooms. If you slipped the mirror along the canal floor with great dexterity, you could see the girls standing under the two showers nearest the dividing wall.

The "authorities," the *metaplot* (plural of metapelet), the youth counselors, and the teachers varied in their responses. I overheard my parents talking about the kids in the tenth grade. My father, who was their physics teacher, said, "At least they will learn something about the laws of optics."

"And if not that, at least about human physiology," my mother, who was an older class's metapelet, said.

But the eight-grade metapelet was livid. She seized a boy in the act of peeking, dragged him out of the boys' side, and, after warning the girls to cover up with towels, thrust him stark naked into their shower.

That story would be my trump card. Surely, my classmates would agree: we had no need to start down this path so early. Nobody had anything new blossoming on their bodies yet, so why now? But our metapelet crushed my mutiny with: "It's said and done." I fumed and acquiesced, but Danny stayed.

A while later I overheard some boys, mostly from the class above us, speaking in hushed tones about going to a hiding place behind the children's house in the afternoon. Something sly about their tones made me eavesdrop. I was flabbergasted when I heard them say they were going with a certain girl from the class below us. *Her? But she is retarded. Why on earth would they include her in their games?*

I cornered Rafi, a close ally within our small class. I thought he would level with me. But when I asked him about the game behind the children's house, he shrugged and pretended he was baffled. I pressed him by alluding to some pretzels he had pilfered from the access-to-grown-ups-only food pantry.

"The boys," he gulped and stopped.

"The boys?" I said.

"They . . ."

"They what?"

"They give her candy or a square of chocolate and she . . ." He looked away.

"And she?" I insisted.

"She takes her clothes off."

"What?"

"She . . . she takes her clothes off so they can see what it looks like."

"But she is retarded!" I yelled.

"Shush!" he warned me, turning red.

"But she's like a four-year-old!"

"I know," he said. "That's why she agrees to do it for two pieces of candy. Sometimes for just one square of chocolate."

I stared at him.

"And nobody says anything?"

"That's how boys are," he said. "It's just how they are. But I don't go with them.

The next day at lunch I announced: "My name is back to Racheli. Call me that and only that."

CHAPTER 12

Drip System

"We should tie her up," Daniel, the biggest among the boys from the fourth grade, said.

A shiver went through me but I clamped my teeth and tightened my fists so it wouldn't show. Maybe I was just chilled. It was early spring and we had just switched from the long-sleeved flannel pajamas to thin cotton short-sleeved ones. Maybe that was why I had woken up in the middle of the night? It was rather unusual. Another shudder fluttered in my gut.

Would they really do that to me? Leave me tied up until morning? I was in third grade, only a year younger than the gang surrounding me—four boys and two girls. But it seemed like an eon at that moment.

I had caught them red-handed in the middle of the night. Getting out of my bed, I saw them dash out of the room, illuminated by the faint light from the hallway. I pretended not to notice and went to the toilet, but on my way back they had caught me. I looked at the kids standing around me in a tight ring now, four boys and two girls.

Some had paintbrushes in their hands, and one girl was holding a watering can.

They had grabbed me on my return from the bathroom, as I crossed the central area, which served as a dining and play room and separated the two wings of the building. Each wing had four bedrooms: three small ones with three beds each, and the last one, at the end of the hallway, a bigger room with four beds. The wing on the right was for us, third graders, and the one on the left was for the fourth grade.

One of the boys surrounding me now in a tight ring was Elik. He was my friend. Our parents' apartments were next to each other on the other side of the kibbutz. We often hung out together in the small pine grove behind them. The excuse had originally been looking for mushrooms in winter. I was in second grade and he in third. But we found we had a lot to talk about, starting with soccer—we were both avid fans of Hapo'el Tel Aviv—but then bigger topics. Should the kibbutz allow private record players in members' homes? Should the kibbutz allow hiring outside laborers? We debated current events in Israel and the world. Do we support the execution of Eichmann even though we oppose the death penalty in principle? Should the American army have supported the Bay of Pigs invasion with more massive force? From the topics of the day we went on to ethical questions and philosophies of life: Are you allowed to steal to feed your hungry family (not that we had any experience of hunger)? Can you lie to save someone from humiliation? Should you live to work or work so you can live?

Elik had said that we should not walk together from the children's house to our parents' in the afternoon. "We don't want the kids to tease us," he explained, "saying we are boyfriend and girlfriend. "Ugh!" I answered, "definitely not!"

I scanned the faces surrounding me in a menacing circle. Elik averted his eyes. The others, girls included, gave me their fiercest stares.

"She'll tell on us in the morning," Ofer, a shorter and chubbier boy, said.

"We'll scare her enough that she won't. Tell her that there'll be hell to pay if she does," Daniel answered. He towered over all of us, but most ominously over me.

"That would work. Do we have any rope?" Ofer asked.

"Does anyone have rope?" Daniel scanned his classmates. No one did. "No rope. So, we can use a sheet." Daniel said.

The boys agreed, and the girls gave vague nods, motions they probably thought could bear a different interpretation come morning.

"Keep her under control," Daniel commanded, and went down the fourth graders' hallway.

At least a sheet won't be as rough as real rope, I thought, comforting myself. But when he came back dragging a sheet behind him, Elik stepped forward. I met his eyes, hopeful—he was my friend, after all.

"There is no need to tie her up. She is a good one. We can trust her. If she promises not to tell, she won't," he said. "Do you promise?" he turned to me.

I couldn't speak, but I nodded. They escorted me to my room, Daniel on one side and Ofer on the other, each gripping my wrist.

"All right, I won't tell," I whispered at the doorway, "but I don't really understand this."

"What?" Elik whispered back.

"I see that you painted some of our faces, and I assume you also tied some kids' sheets. We know those tricks. But what's this thing with the cans of water in the middle of the room?"

"That's the best part!" Daniel said, so proud he forgot to whisper.

"It is?"

"If you hear water dripping while you are asleep, you'll pee in your bed. So tomorrow morning all of you—pathetic third graders—will wake up having wet your beds."

"Yea! That will be something," one of the girls said.

"Really?"

"Yes! We read it in a magazine," Daniel said and released his hold on my wrist. I shuffled to my bed and slid under the covers. All the warmth I had accumulated in the course of the night had dissipated. The frigid sheets accelerated my shivers.

I thought I wouldn't sleep all night. I couldn't stop listening to the drip-drip of the water on the bottom of the tin can. I felt the urge to go to the bathroom again and again, but didn't dare. But I must have fallen asleep at some point because I awoke to the metapelet's cheery "Good morning, children." There was nothing in the middle of the room. The contraption was gone. The fourth graders must have dismantled it before dawn.

Two of the kids in my room woke up with their faces painted in brown and black shoe polish, and the third needed help yanking her feet out of the tightly knotted sheet. The same scene greeted the kids in the other rooms. Yells and curses bounced from room to room. I jumped out of bed and rushed to the bathroom, praying none of the other kids noticed that I had been visited by neither trick. I washed my face for a long time, using plenty of soap, hoping the girls at the sink on either side of me assumed that, like them, I was removing the paint from my cheeks and forehead.

But the *coup de grâce* came to naught. Not one of us third graders woke up in a wet bed. I was elated . . . but mum. As the metapelet ranted during our breakfast and threatened to find out who was responsible, I tried to catch some fourth graders' eyes but no one returned my glance. They all feigned ignorance of the crime and the culprit. Two of them fingered the seventh graders while Daniel implicated the group of teenage city kids from troubled homes who were schooled at the kibbutz and lived in their own dormitories. Some of them had been juvenile delinquents, he said with a knowing nod.

Finally the metapelet rushed us to finish breakfast and go to our classrooms. I passed Elik on the way out.

"Thank you," I whispered.

"Thank *you*," he whispered back.

"It wasn't easy . . ." we murmured in unison.

* * *

"It wasn't easy" became a code between us, even as our friendship drifted away with the passing years. Sometimes we said it in earnest, as when our soccer team (we both played defense) got trounced 9–1 by the team from a neighboring kibbutz; other times, sarcastically— as after the eighth-grade national proficiency exam (we were both excellent students). Sometimes we applied it to an impending event. Before the Six-Day War, while digging trenches on the school grounds as the country was gripped by cataclysmic fears, we passed each other and muttered to each other, "This will not be easy."

When Elik tried out for one of the most selective units of the Israel Defense Forces, he passed me at the dining hall on Erev Shabbat, mouthing, "That was not easy." But then he smiled and two weeks later everyone on the kibbutz knew he had been accepted. We kept tabs on each other that way, he through his grueling army service, I through a pre-army year as a youth movement counselor in Tel Aviv and an easy, if not cushy, service. All we needed to say was "Not easy" or "Not so easy."

Elik was killed on the Golan Heights during the Yom Kippur War, over forty years ago. I still think about him often. It has not been easy.

CHAPTER 13

Her Mother

"Children, listen now," the third-grade teacher said in a somber tone when we took our seats after the ten o'clock recess. "You all have to be extra good friends to Aliza now."

Had we done something wrong? I wondered. My mind raced through a short list of things we had done together recently, Aliza, me, and Nitza, the third in our trio. Nothing untoward.

I stole a glance around the room. Suddenly our small two-person desks appeared disheveled, the tops littered with pencils, erasers, and open notebooks. I noticed three pieces of crumpled paper in the far corner and that the blackboard was smeared with chalk streaks. Everyone straightened their back and watched the teacher closely.

"It's terribly sad," she finally continued, "but you all need to know that her mother died today. All of you have to think about how you could help Aliza."

There was a stunned silence.

"Aliza's mother?" I braved the question, though I had heard it loud and clear.

"Yes. Marion. Early this morning in the hospital in Afula."

No one knew what to say, so we just nodded. I was on my own figuring it out. If only I knew what being a good friend entailed in such circumstances. Do you say something about it or stay silent? Are you allowed to say Marion's name now that she's dead? The teacher gave us no further instructions.

I actually had a relationship with Marion beyond the fact that she was my friend's mother. Several years earlier, I had had a concussion and, on doctors' orders, had to lie flat in bed for two weeks, motionless, if possible. Let the brain rest, I suppose was the logic of medical know-how at the time; stop any vibrating and jiggling so it can heal.

I had to stay at my parents' apartment instead of the children's house so I could be strictly supervised and not be tempted to move when my friends played and ran around. Marion came to my bedside every morning to keep me occupied. My parents had to go to their jobs. It made perfect sense within the context of kibbutz education. Expert caretakers—metaplot—not their parents, took care of kids all day. When we were sick, too. Normally, if we were down with something contagious, we would spend the day in *"izolatziyah,"* a dedicated isolation sick room in the children's house. But there was too much horsing around, even among the sick kids, to keep me there. I would never be able to lie there motionless all day.

I suppose Marion read me stories but I don't remember those. I only remember the craft projects, a knotted-twine key chain (though nobody on the kibbutz needed keys—nothing was ever locked), a woven potholder, and a small raffia basket.

At the time, I had thought she was assigned this job because she was particularly patient. It seemed to go with her personality—delicate to the point of frailty, timid, even to the point of seeming feeble. Suddenly, when the teacher said she had died, I understood: she had already been sick then. She had already been battling the cancer that had now won.

"Of course, I'll be her friend," I assured the teacher as the class filed out at the end of the lesson. "I am already her good friend. But what, what actually am I supposed to do?"

"Just be her friend. Just be like always."

"Just as usual?" I was confused.

"Yes," the teacher said. "You'll see what happens, what she wants to talk about, what she wants to do."

I nodded as if I understood, but inside I could already feel a trembling. Sure, I was proud to be one of those chosen for this special assignment. I felt it in my upper chest—it lifted just a bit. But my stomach was already in knots, protesting that I had no idea what I should say or do. I had never talked to anyone whose mother had died. Or father. Or any family member. Nobody died on the kibbutz. All our parents were, after all, young people, in their thirties and forties. There were almost no grandparents, no old people. They had all died in Europe, but nobody talked about it in front of us kids.

"You can go out to recess now," the teacher said and put her hand on my shoulder for a brief moment. I walked outside and looked at my friends playing. Lucky ones . . . they didn't know yet. I leaned against the wall that had stored soothing warmth from the rays of the morning sun, but an icy mass in the pit of my stomach made me shiver. I scanned the yard looking for Aliza. She wasn't there. I lifted my eyes and saw her a hundred paces down the path, the kibbutz nurse holding her hand and talking to her as they walked away. Aliza's reed-thin legs, which I had always envied, seemed spindly and weak, and her two long braids (another source of envy) had lost their bounce.

I stayed pressed against the wall until the teacher called us back to class. When everyone was seated quietly at their desks she told the kids about Aliza's mother. She added that the funeral would be in the afternoon, and a substitute would stay with us, because our metapelet had been a close friend of Marion and had to go to the cemetery. We would stay in the children's house an extra hour since the funeral would be at four, right after everyone finished their work duties in the fields.

"Aliza will be staying with her family for a day or two," the teacher went on, "and when she comes back to the children's house you all have to be extra nice to her."

"Of course."

"We know."

Two days later Aliza came back to the children's house, and we all reminded each other to treat her nicely, but normally, as if nothing had changed. In the afternoon, when it was time to go home I asked if she wanted to walk together. Our parents' apartments were near each other. We often walked home together and played in what we called "The Pine Grove," really just a double row of rather spindly pines planted ten years earlier behind the row of houses. In the winter we would look for mushrooms growing under those trees, and in the summer, for a little bit of shade.

"Do you want to play something?" I asked when we got near our parents' houses.

"Yes, but what can we play?" she asked and shrugged her bony shoulders.

"Well, we can't, I mean it wouldn't be right to play hopscotch," I said. Hopscotch was the current fad; we played it for hours every day, at the children's house and at our parents'.

"No," she said.

I could hear the quiver in her voice. It oscillated at the same frequency as the tremor in my diaphragm.

"Nothing with jumping," I said. "Jumping wouldn't be right."

"No," she agreed.

"So no jump rope, either." I extrapolated. "I guess hide-and-seek would not be right, either?"

"I don't think so."

Suddenly I realized that Aliza had no idea either; she was winging it just like I was.

But it was my job to be nice to her, to play with her, so I had to come up with something.

"We can play marbles," I suggested. "That's sitting down."

"Well . . . I am not sure we should play outside already. It's less than a week."

"You are right," I said, embarrassed that I didn't know the unspoken protocol.

So we played five-stones in the small room of my parents' apartment. I was glad I wasn't that good at the game because I didn't have to try to let her win. Then we played cards and dominos. My mother poked her head into the room.

"You should go home now, Aliza. It's getting late." She nodded and left without another word.

After a week of playing indoor games, I brought up marbles again.

"Yes . . . It's . . . fine now. And . . . probably no one will see us." Aliza spoke slowly, as if getting each word out of her mouth required lifting a huge rock that blocked its way. We found a spot under one of the pine trees behind my parents' house where the ground was hard and smooth enough for the game. There were already three small hollows dug in there, from previous games. I cleaned out the dirt and pine needles that had accumulated inside and around them, not minding the grit wedging itself under my fingernails. Aliza just watched me prepare the ground, not lifting a finger, as if her hands were useless twigs, suspended from her shoulders.

We settled down on the hard ground and I opened my bag of marbles.

"You can choose any marbles you want," I said, rolling out my small collection.

"You can even keep them," I added.

"No," she said. "I have my own."

"But not here, right?"

"No," she shook her head. "I'll borrow yours. I don't want to go home."

"You don't want to go home?" I asked and must have frowned for an instant before rearranging my face into a pleasant smile, because she hastened to add: "I mean right now. To get the marbles."

"Of course," I said, but I was pretty sure I heard her right the first time.

We played outside for a long time until I heard my mother calling me. I invited Aliza to come in with me and get a cold drink.

"All right," she said. "Just for a minute."

Inside, we sat quietly on the edge of the bed that served as a couch during the day. My mother brought out tall glasses of berry juice. It was made with ersatz concentrate, but it was still a treat, especially with the added flair of wax-paper straws. Usually we drank plain cold water, straight out of the glass. Usually I served myself.

We didn't say much. Just "The juice is good" and "Thank you." As we sipped the juice slowly, my mother sat down next to Aliza.

"You are always welcome to come here," she said in a near whisper. "And if you have any questions, you can always ask me."

Aliza didn't say anything, but I thought she gave a small nod. Maybe she had just bent her head down to take the final sip of juice. Then she cleared her throat and said in a near-whisper: "Just one question."

"Yes?" my mother said softly and sat down next to her.

Aliza still hesitated.

"It's all right," my mother said. "You can ask me anything."

"Where is she?" Aliza blurted out, then clamped her lips shut.

"She is in her grave. In the cemetery."

"No," Aliza said. "I know about . . . about the body. I mean . . . where is *she,* like she was when she was my mother."

"Aha," my mother said and put her hand on Aliza's shoulder. "The person she was is inside you, inside everyone who knew her. When you, or anyone else, remembers her, when you . . . all of us, think about her."

Aliza nodded in silence. After another minute she stood up.

"I have to go home now," she said.

"Just one minute," I said to her. I'd been thinking about this for a while. Now seemed to be the right time.

"I have something from your . . . your . . . from her." I couldn't bring myself to say "mother."

"Come," I said and walked over to the shelf that held my books and a few toys. I took down the small raffia basket and showed it to Aliza. She gave me a puzzled look.

"She made this with me. When I had a concussion a few years ago."

I put it in Aliza's hand. She ran her finger along the thin raffia strands. They were still shiny and smooth.

"But it's yours," she said. I could see a tear gathering in each of the corners of her eyes.

"No. I was three years old then," I said shaking my head. "She, she really is the one who made it."

Aliza turned the basket this way and that. She clenched her jaw. Her eyes were wet. I could tell she was fighting to keep the tears from rolling down.

"No, you keep it," she handed it back to me.

"Are you sure?"

"Yes," she said, with that quiver in her voice again.

"If you have it here, she'll be in more places. If other people see it . . . she'll be here, too."

CHAPTER 14

Night Walk

"Your turn," Dinah said and gave me a small nudge. She held the rusty iron gate wide open. My stomach seized and I took two small gulps of air. I could feel the puffs get stuck in my throat. But I couldn't admit my fear, let alone show it, not to my classmates and not to myself. I clamped my teeth to stop their chattering and looked out, past the barbed wire fence that surrounded and protected the kibbutz.

The boys had gone first, the destination our *"machaneh,"* an encampment in a hidden spot in the steep gully leading to the Jordan River, nestled between the graveyard and Giv'at Ha-Kalaniyot, where every winter a cluster of anemones gave the hilltop a red crown. We had cleared a small area of thistles and brush and built simple benches from eucalyptus branches, in a circle around a fire pit where we held weekly adventures.

Up until now we had always made the ten-minute walk from the edge of the kibbutz to our encampment in a group, and mostly in daylight. We had practiced for weeks: approaching a target first crouching, then "Indian style," crawling on our stomachs; camouflaging ourselves with small leafy branches; finding our way blind-folded with old rags. It was never fully explained why, in fourth grade, we needed to undertake this paramilitary training. After all, we still had eight or nine years before we'd join the army, and even our counselors, Gidi and Dinah, were still four years shy of induction. It was just something you had to master, of a piece with other methods to toughen us up and make us fearless.

Going alone to the machaneh, in the dark, was the culmination of those weeks of training. When each of us would reach the encampment, where Gidi would be waiting for us, we would have proven ourselves. After everyone had arrived, we were going to have a celebration: make coffee in a *finjan* over the fire pit (real coffee, not the pretend coffee we drank every day, which had a thimbleful of coffee in a quart of boiled milk) and roasted potatoes on the coals. And ghost stories too—a delicious make-believe-fear after we'd overcome the real thing.

I had volunteered to be the first girl, to set an example for the others who were not afraid to say they were scared. "Being an example" was almost a religion with us. And what was there to be scared of, anyway? "Nothing," Gidi had said when he explained our mission the week before. He would wait for us at the camp while Dinah stayed by the gate, then follow the last of us to set out, making sure everyone made it. There was going to be a three-quarter moon, so we would have no problem seeing the road, and, anyway, by now we all knew the path by heart.

But there was plenty to worry about. First, the most obvious: the dark. Three-quarter moon or not, it was still going to be the scary black of night. But that you couldn't admit. Being frightened of the dark was for little kids, and I could convince myself I was not afraid of it. Secondly, snakes—those were real, poisonous, and everywhere. That was a legitimate fear, but I was wearing my high-top shoes. That should take care of it.

But I was still nervous. *Just walk really fast*, I told myself—no, run! The snakes wouldn't be able to get you if you were really fast. Same for the scorpions that might be out there, though we had been told that those stayed under their rocks and wouldn't bother you if you didn't remove their cover.

So there was a moon, and I was wearing my high-tops, and I was going to run. All set? No, because my real fear was *mistanenim*, infiltrators from Jordan. There had actually been an incident, about a year earlier. One night I awoke to go to the bathroom, and in the hallway I heard shouts and fast footsteps outside. I ran back to my bed. Thank God Sammi was awake and whispered to me: "Be quiet! Hide under your blanket and don't move!" I pulled the covers over my head. I tried to breathe as quietly as I could. After a minute the voices and footsteps faded away.

"What happened?" I whispered to Sammi.

"*Mistanenim,*" he whispered back.

"*Imma-leh!*" I gasped.

"Or maybe just thieves," Sammi said, trying to calm me down.

I lay awake—I thought all night—but I suppose I did fall asleep because suddenly it was daylight and the metapelet was waking us up for breakfast. While we ate our scrambled eggs, the kibbutz security officer came in. He was wearing khakis that looked like a uniform of some sort and had noticeable stubble. Clearly, he hadn't had time to shave this morning. We'd never seen him wear anything during the day but the regular dark blue or gray work clothes everyone wore. We all straightened our backs and hushed, all eyes on him.

"Two infiltrators were caught overnight by the night guards," he began, "but don't be afraid. There will be twice as many guards from now on, and soldiers too." He repeated several times that we were safe, but added that if we ever woke up at night and heard suspicious sounds, we should hide under our blankets and keep totally still.

"Never get out of your beds, and never, ever, go to the window to look out," he concluded and left.

Sammi and I became instant heroes: we had heard the shouts and the footsteps. In our telling and retelling, the shouts included words in Arabic, and Sammi had seen shadowy figures wearing *keffiyehs* running past the windows.

But that had been over a year and a half ago. When, during the preparation session, Sammi asked about it, Gidi assured us there was nothing to worry about. "There aren't any mistanenim anymore." I wanted so much to be fearless, as Gidi was exhorting us to be. I wanted so much to be as brave as he was. We all saw him as the epitome of vigor and courage, though it was years before he would join the army and serve in the Sayeret Matkal, the most elite unit of the Israel Defense Forces.

I had made myself feel brave by loudly reassuring the other kids in my class. I had repeated it the whole week—"There are no infiltrators anymore"—over and over until this moment. And now I had to step out past the gate.

I looked back at the girls lined up behind me. They whispered among themselves about how frightened they were. I was simultaneously contemptuous and envious of them—for being scaredy-cats and for being able to say they were afraid. Fear was such a confusing thing! We were raised by "You mustn't be afraid." We were also supposed to always be honest. There was no bridging between the two.

I darted out the gate. As long as the girls and Dinah could still see me, I walked. Briskly, yes, but I walked, trying to hold my head high in what I imagined courage looked like. Once I was swallowed by the dark, I ran. I was not much of a sprinter, but I sure ran fast that night. And even though we had been instructed to practice all the skills we had learned for proceeding in silence and making stealth movements in the dark, I talked out loud the whole time. I tried to sing—a heroic military march—but my voice cracked. All I could do was recite out loud: "There are no infiltrators anymore. There are no infiltrators anymore."

I am sure I got there safely, though I don't remember my arrival. So did the rest of the girls, the last ones allowed to go in pairs. I am

sure we had our celebration and real coffee and coal-blackened potatoes. But I don't remember that either.

Years later I was reminiscing with Gidi about our exciting adventures back in fourth grade. "Remember the time we walked alone to
our machaneh in the gully under the cemetery?" I asked, quite certain he would have no idea what I was talking about.

"Do I remember?" he exclaimed. "I was so terrified waiting for all
of you there at the encampment, all alone in the dark, what with the
mistanenim scare and all that . . ."

CHAPTER 15

Snakes and Kisses

The whole problem was due to the snakes and the occasional scorpion. Poisonous, of course. In summer they would slither out of their hiding places in the late afternoon and settle themselves for a tummy warming on the paved sidewalks, which had stored heat all day under the blazing sun. We mostly walked barefoot or in sandals all summer, so snakes were a big concern. Our parents and caretakers warned us never to go barefoot in the evening. They didn't much worry about daytime, when we were likely to step on all manner of thorns, rusty nails, and occasionally glass shards. All of those could be pulled out with a pair of tweezers, and we'd all had our tetanus shots. The adults did not know about our favorite summer sport: running barefoot from the pool to the children's house on the dirt path, with an inch-thick layer of fine, scorching dust. We'd burn the tender skin right under and between our toes, but it would heal by the next day. Halfway through the summer, the skin had toughened enough so that it no longer bled. It also proved thick enough against most thorns.

But snakes they did worry about. Of course—a viper bite on your foot would kill you in thirty minutes. Higher up—closer to your heart—each centimeter cut your margin by a minute. Every two to three weeks a story would circulate throughout the whole kibbutz about another viper killed in the nick of time, usually with a long-handle hoe. A blow delivered swiftly and accurately would separate the snake's head from its body before it struck with its deadly fangs. As the story raced from mouth to ear, the size of the snake grew, from the typical one to two feet, to gargantuan four-foot creatures. At the same rate, but in inverse proportion, the distance between the snake's head and the nearly-struck victim's foot, hand, or backside (of the fool who sat on a rock that a snake had favored) shrank.

We knew our parents were right, but there was a logical paradox. If you left the children's house at 4:30 p.m. barefoot, as we usually did, and forgot to tote along your sandals, what were you to do at dusk, when the looming evening reminded you of the forgotten sandals? Run back to the children's house barefoot to retrieve the sandals and then be safe—or at least a bit safer—in the event that you stepped on a snake after nightfall? Hadn't the snakes already slithered out of their holes by then? One solution was to bike to the children's house, but our old, battered bikes were often disabled by flat tires (caused by the same thorns afflicting our bare feet). This approach lost favor after a kibbutz member was startled by a snake coiled around his bike's handlebar.

I tried to remember to take my sandals with me every afternoon. My mother would check on it when I arrived home. If I'd forgotten, she'd send me right back, admonishing me to scan the paved sidewalk several feet ahead before I took a step. Who could walk that slowly? But I was, indeed, petrified of those vipers. Everyone knew they proliferated on the mostly abandoned Giv'ah, the hill on the edge of the kibbutz, where I had to go to practice piano. The piano room was at the bottom floor of the water tower, the highest point of the Giv'ah.

The Giv'ah was where the kibbutz had originally started in 1938, a minuscule "settlement" of a few small one-story buildings and a wooden watchtower surrounded by a stockade. Our kibbutz was one of the many "stockade and tower" (*Homah U-Migdal*) outposts established overnight in the late thirties and early forties. There were severe restrictions on the number of new Jewish settlements the British Mandate permitted each year, but there was a loophole—an old Ottoman regulation, part of the Ottoman jurisprudence that still governed much of domestic law in Palestine: a house built illegally could not be torn down if by the time it was discovered it already had four walls and a roof. Dozens of new kibbutzim were thus built overnight, as ours was. Walls and roof segments, parts of the stockade, and sections of the wooden watchtower were all assembled in advance over several weeks in a nearby kibbutz. In our case, it was Ma'oz Chayim, four kilometers up the road. On the set date, hundreds of people (those creating the new kibbutz, members of Ma'oz, and many volunteers from neighboring settlements) trudged down the road in the middle of the night, carrying these large wooden segments on a few trucks and tractors, and by a long row of hands. They arrived at our Kfar Ruppin hill before dawn and started erecting the structures. In full daylight, the neighboring Bedouins saw what was happening and alerted the British police. By the time they arrived, several buildings had walls and roofs—too late for a tear-down and eviction order.

A few years later, the rickety wooden tower was replaced by a solid cement water tower, the pride of the kibbutz. It had two one-room floors, above them a two-story-high water tank, and on top a guard post with floodlights. Two flagpoles crowned the tower: one with an Israeli flag (flown every day) and one with the workers' red flag, unfurled on holidays and on May Day well into the early sixties.

The bottom floor was the piano room, where I went to practice for my lessons, starting in fifth grade. Beside the piano, there was room only for one chair tucked against its side, a piano bench, and a small

I am practicing in the Kfar Ruppin piano room.

bookcase for music books. The air in the room was bone chilling in winter, so I played in my heavy jacket. In summer it was surprisingly pleasant. The very thick cement walls held the coolness of night until the following evening. At night the walls shed the stored heat. In the wee hours they began storing up the coolness again.

It was over 100 degrees outside, but I asked my mother to dig up my winter rubber boots to wear when I went to practice piano. My mother blew my mind: she praised me for telling her I was scared! She told me it was perfectly reasonable; it was, in fact, wise to be afraid of snakes lurking on that hill. She pulled the boots from the storage drawer. They came up to my knees—no snake could get that high. My feet swam in sweat inside the boots as I hiked up the hill in the afternoon's nearly 100-degree heat, but I didn't care one bit. I was snake-proof. It would have been a lethal embarrassment if anyone in my class saw me, so I took a circuitous route and approached the hill from the far, untraveled side. I put the boots on after making sure there was no one in sight.

Safe from snakes, I merrily trudged up the hill, wholly ignorant of another danger; this danger connected to snakes too, but only through the mythopoeic gaze of the Bible.

* * *

It was a very hot July afternoon, so I decided to skip the usual soccer game and go practice piano instead, earlier than usual. All the kids in my class had rushed home to beg their parents to take them to the pool, so I didn't need to follow my usual circuitous route, and I walked up the hill directly from the children's house.

I perked up my ears to see if I heard the piano from outside. There was a much older girl, an eleventh grader, who also played piano. We had no system for taking turns practicing, other than listening to see if either of us was already inside playing. I wasn't surprised that it was quiet; she usually played much later than me, often at night, after she had finished her much heavier load of homework.

I was humming my Clementi exercises as I reached the door and swung it wide open. I froze, my mouth half open. Sitting on the piano keyboard was that girl. Kneeling on the bench tucked as close into the piano as possible was her boyfriend. His hands were inside her shirt, the two of them entwined in a luscious kiss. For a moment it seemed like they didn't even realize I was there. *Run!* my head screamed, but my legs were momentarily nailed to the floor. I held my breath. Finally, she pulled her face back and gave me a nod that meant, "Scram."

I did, running faster than I ever had on account of snakes or scorpions. At the bottom of the hill I stopped and waited for my breath to steady and my heart's beating to subside. I touched my face: red hot. I knew it was from what I had seen, not from running. I found an irrigation hose and wet my face to cool it down, then walked slowly home, composing myself before I arrived.

"You came straight home," my mother said with some surprise when I got to my parents' room. "Yes," I blurted out. "It . . . it's really hot. Let's go to the pool."

That night I dug in the back of my drawer and pulled out the child's harmonica I had disdained since I started piano lessons. I played it with all my might every time I went up the hill to the piano room.

CHAPTER 16

Shabbat and Sacrilege

Sunset meant Shabbat was about to start, and I was now marooned on this religious kibbutz until I could see three stars the next evening. That meant about twenty-five hours of comporting myself with the religious requirements of Shabbat: no lights turned on or off, no writing, no driving or bike riding, and no listening to the radio — all the typical things I would do on Shabbat at home. A bit of a pain, but all right, I thought, it'll be a novel experience. How hard could it be?

Spending Shabbat at a religious kibbutz was one of the twelve tasks that made up my individual bat mitzvah challenge. Each of us in our seventh-grade class chose twelve tasks, out of a list of twenty options, to complete over the school year. The year would culminate with group bar/bat mitzvah celebrations in June. Our whole class would stage a performance with slides of childhood photographs, skits, and songs we wrote to celebrate the occasion. In our secular, kibbutz-style bar and bat mitzvah we did not go near a Torah; we memorized no prayers and learned no Torah-chanting trope. Rather, we had to complete twelve tasks, which represented entry into adult responsibilities expected on a kibbutz, such as working an eight-hour day in one of the kibbutz branches, teaching a class in the lower grade of the elementary school, or taking on a dusk-to-dawn guard duty with the night watchmen.

Paired with this coming of age moment were also a wristwatch and new clothes. This was a huge leap for us: no one under twelve owned a wristwatch and it was not acceptable to buy one on your own (nor really affordable). You waited patiently until the kibbutz granted you this token of adulthood. There was only one style of watch, one size for the boys, and a slightly daintier one, though with an extremely simple design, for the girls. For our new clothes there was also a new privilege: we could each choose a floral print fabric from an array offered by the kibbutz seamstress, who would sew us a custom-made dress shirt: "boat neck" style for the girls and button down for the boys. Up until now we'd choose every season from ready-made clothes in plain colors or checkered, at best. Even more exciting were store-bought pants. Since most of our clothing was sewn on the kibbutz, ready-to-wear was a luxury. The color was going to be cream—so sophisticated! Up till now all our pants had been gray, dark blue, or khaki. Jeans were not even a glimmer in our eye.

I went to the religious kibbutz with great anticipation: it was the last task on my list. I had already spent a whole night with the night watchman patrolling the paths of the kibbutz, worked a full eight-hour day in the dining room serving breakfast and lunch, and, in between, cleaned all forty or so three-foot-high windows. I had also sailed through my "Robinson Crusoe Day," camped alone in the area outside the kibbutz that we called "The Jungle." It was a grove of huge eucalyptus trees and overgrown reeds and weeds along a trickle of a stream north of the road leading to the kibbutz. I had set out before breakfast with provisions to make my own meals. I was not allowed to take a book, a transistor radio, or a watch. When I heard the four o'clock bus drive by, I was allowed to come out of the bush and back to civilization.

Perhaps the most daunting task was to go to "the City," in my case Haifa, with a list of four things to buy for members of the kibbutz. I ticked off the steps in my head: take the bus by myself, switch to the right second bus in the central station in Afula, get off at the right place in Haifa (that meant asking the driver to tell me when—so embarrassing!), find four different stores, and pay the correct amount from the small purse the kibbutz treasurer had given me. The one purchase I remember was four buttons. I had a piece of cardboard with a button sewn onto it: I was to find the exact replica.

The stay in a religious kibbutz, located only three kilometers from ours, stood in contrast to a two-day visit, a month earlier, to the Ha-Shomer Ha-Tza'ir kibbutz an hour away (another, even more complicated set of bus rides on my own). At Ha-Shomer (further left on the political spectrum than our kibbutz), it was rumored, boys and girls our age still showered together. It was on account of their extremist communitarianism. I had taken an extra-long shower the day before my departure, figuring I could get through two days without one. But how would I explain it to my hosts?

When I got there I was profoundly relieved: they did not shower together anymore. They only shared rooms—two boys and two girls in each room in their Beit Yeladim. That was a snap: I could change in and out of my pajamas under my blanket. The local girls just ordered the boys to turn around. Everything else was pretty much the same as at our kibbutz, so it turned out to be one of the easiest tasks on my list.

At first glance, when I arrived in the mid-afternoon at the religious kibbutz, it looked the same as ours, except the men and boys wore *kippot*. The girl hosting me showed me to a girls-only room and helped me settle on a bed with a small side cabinet that looked exactly like mine back home. Everyone dressed up in white shirts for Shabbat eve. That, too, was just like at home.

"First we go to the synagogue," she explained, "and then after prayers to the *chadar ochel* for dinner."

"Just like us . . . eh . . . without the synagogue," I said nonchalantly, trying to disguise the fact that I had never been to a synagogue
and knew little of what would transpire there.

At the synagogue I stood next to my host and her sisters, holding
the *siddur* and turning the pages in sync with them. I lip-synched as
the whole community chanted and sang. I had no idea why and when
they would stand up or sit down, read in silence, switch to a murmur,
read out loud, or repeat after the *chazzan*. But I could fake it pretty
easily. The singing undulated between soft, almost mournful, melo-
dies and a rollicking "Lekhah Dodi," welcoming the Shabbat. The
melody was the same one we sang at my kibbutz dining room before
Friday night's dinner, but there were many more verses, which I had
never known about.

The whole community walked slowly from the synagogue to the
nearby chadar ochel, singing and exchanging "Shabbat Shalom"
greetings. They took their seats and began a new song. Then another,
and another. It was a lot more harmonious and pleasing than the
ruckus at my kibbutz at Friday night dinners. The food was pretty
much the same as ours: chicken so overcooked it was nearly tasteless
(we called it "laundered chicken"—every ounce of flavor had been
washed out), boiled potatoes, and finely chopped salad. Despite my
general ignorance about Jewish law, I knew enough not to expect the
ice cream we so looked forward to at home. Instead they had cake
that had the similar suffocatingly dry density as our kibbutz-produced
cakes. There was a popular joke circulating that it was the murder
weapon in a violent domestic dispute at an unnamed kibbutz.

After dinner, the seventh grade gathered in the Beit Yeladim for
their regular Erev Shabbat activity. Whereas at our kibbutz that was
usually listening to music and attempting to learn the steps of popular dances, for them it was a discussion of Parashat Ha-Shavu'a, the
weekly Torah portion to be chanted in synagogue the next day. The
discussion quickly homed in on what was God's plan and intention.
The various ideas soon generated a lively debate. Deep into it, the
counselor leading the discussion turned to me and said enthusiasti-

cally, "Let's hear from our guest. What do you think God intended here? How does what we humans do look in God's eye?"

"It's a meaningless question," I blurted out before my internal censor had a chance to stop me, "since there is no God." An ice-cold silence engulfed the room. The counselor was pressing his lips together, clearly stopping himself from saying the words about to burst out of his mouth. I scanned the room: wide eyes, mouths hanging open, fingers fidgeting. Finally, the counselor spoke: "Well, that's certainly a different opinion from ours." He looked around the room but clearly no one knew what to say. "Well, then," he continued, "it's getting late so we'll end here." Everyone bolted out of the room.

I was the last one to leave, not sure where I should go now. "Where do we go now?" I asked the counselor who closed the door behind us (without turning the light off, I noted to myself).

"Everyone goes to his or her own room," he said, "and you . . . you are lucky that it's Shabbat so we can't drive you. You'd be halfway home by now, believe me!"

Thankfully, it was close to bedtime and day one was over. Time crawled on Shabbat as after morning prayers and lunch I hung out with everyone in the class and we all tried to find subjects to talk about that had nothing to do with God. I couldn't wait for three stars to come out and for my ride back home to arrive.

* * *

Years later my mother had a colleague from that same kibbutz. They worked together at the family therapy clinic that served all the kibbutzim in the region——secular, religious, far left, and middle of the road. She invited my mother several times to spend Shabbat with her and her husband. "It's very beautiful," she said, "especially Erev Shabbat prayers and dinner and the Shabbat morning. And you don't have to stay for the full service," she assured my mother, who, at that point in her more than eighty years had never been to a Shabbat service in a synagogue.

Finally, my mother agreed and went to her colleague's on Friday in the late afternoon. She found the Friday night service and communal dinner lovely, indeed. Even the Shabbat morning service, while seeming endless to her, was punctuated by beautiful singing and bathed in a special spirit. After lunch, back at the apartment, they relaxed in comfortable armchairs. The husband got up and put on a record of Bach's *Unaccompanied Cello Suites*.

"How can you do this?" my mother asked. "Isn't it against the law, a desecration of Shabbat?"

"No," he said firmly, "listening to Bach, even on Shabbat, couldn't possibly be a desecration in God's eye."

CHAPTER 17

Eighth-Grade Baby

I headed to the Beit Yeladim early in the evening because I had left the novel I was reading there. It was a good read, so having finished my homework early I thought I'd go back for a half hour of deliciously quiet reading until everyone else arrived. As I approached the building I noticed my room, shared with three other girls at the far end of the hallway, was dimly lit. *I must have forgotten to turn off my small reading lamp,* I thought to myself.

I entered the Beit Yeladim and went down the hallway, my mind already scrolling to the last sentence I had read in my book. I flung the door open and heard a strange mix of moans and gasps. I froze. *Someone in the room! Some kind of intruder?* I was years past my fears of "infiltrators," but still, on a dark night, alone in the Beit Yeladim . . . I scanned the room from my bed at the far wall to Shoshi's right by the door. Aha! She was there. And someone was on top of her, his bare back glistening with sweat. The tail end of a loud moan hovered over him.

"Got to go to the bathroom," I called out as I slammed the door shut. I ran down the hallway.

A few minutes later, allowing for the normal interval for a bathroom trip, I entered again. This time, Shoshi was clutching the covers she'd pulled up to her chin. Her boyfriend perched on the edge of the bed, the bedspread twisted and bunched against his groin. He was fully dressed but barefoot, a bit odd as it was winter and the room was chilly. I saw his shoes and socks lurking under the bed on the cold tile floor. I averted my eyes and said nothing, until the silence became intolerable.

"Did you finish your homework already?" I asked Shoshi as if everything was normal.

She opened her mouth but no words came out.

"I did," I said to fill the void.

"Yes, earlier," Shoshi finally managed.

Now I could look at her, still trying to seem completely nonchalant. Her face was flushed, a film of perspiration shone on her upper lip, and she was grasping the blankets so tightly her knuckles popped.

"I, I, I'm going now," her boyfriend stammered, pushed his feet into his shoes without bothering with the socks, and ran off.

"I came early to read my book," I suddenly felt I had to explain myself.

Shoshi nodded. She gave me a long look that I knew meant, "Don't tell anyone." I nodded back. Of course I wouldn't betray her. If anything, I felt ashamed for seeing them.

After that evening, I always whistled or sang loudly when I entered the Beit Yeladim and found it still deserted. I'd cough a couple of times while still at the far end of the corridor from my room and walk down very slowly. If the door was closed I'd knock—something we never did. Usually there was no one in the room. If Shoshi and her boyfriend were there, they'd be sitting on top of the bedspread, looking at a book or seemingly doing homework.

Shoshi and I were closest in age in our group of twelve. We were both fourteen, but she was a couple of months older than me. But we were never very friendly. I didn't have anything against her, but I loathed her father. Back in kindergarten he terrified me in a dream.

In it, I am sitting in the anteroom of my parents' two-room apartment playing with the wood box my father had made for me. Shoshi's father barges in and steps right over me. Before I can call out he lunges at my mother and yanks her up by her hair. He pulls so hard he yanks her up to standing. The dream, or at least my memory of it, ends right then in a moment of terror.

I held it against him my whole childhood. I must have sensed something menacing in him. He was a Holocaust survivor, "from the camps," as we overheard grown-ups whisper behind his back, raising their eyebrows to explain some aberration in his behavior. Unlike most of the kibbutz members, he never worked in the fields. Instead he drove a truck, so big and powerful it was a bit scary to our child-eyes. We knew to stay out of his way; he was rumored to be quick with the slaps. Her mother was so quiet and mousy that no one took any notice of her. She worked silently, mending socks and undershirts.

But I tried not to hold the frightening dream against Shoshi herself. Sometimes I even bent over backwards to be nice to her and include her in our group activities. She was not among the popular kids in our class; she didn't excel in anything and didn't have her niche in the group. Her only claim to fame was because of one eye: the iris that was split horizontally, half brown and half green.

* * *

A few months later, the metapelet called us one afternoon for a class meeting. We assembled in the dining room where we ate our breakfast and afternoon snacks.

"It's about Shoshi," the metapelet started while we were still chatting with each other. "Something very grave has happened to her." My breath froze. Everyone hushed and looked around the room, now realizing we hadn't noticed that Shoshi was not there.

Is Shoshi seriously ill? Did she die? Or one of her parents? Or . . . what?

"Shoshi has gotten pregnant," the metapelet said in a disapproving tone. "She will be having a baby in two months."

We exchanged shocked glances. I felt my face go pale. Somehow I was guilty in this. I should have done something after that evening, should have told my mother. She could have helped Shoshi, prevented her from falling into the dark pit she was in now. My mother was the kind of person on the kibbutz one could go to in delicate situations.

"Because of that," the metapelet continued, "she can no longer live in the Beit Yeladim and won't be going to school with the rest of you."

No one thought to ask why. We just nodded as the metapelet continued on, telling us we would have a sex education class soon. We'd had it in fourth grade and sixth grade; we should have known everything, but clearly Shoshi did not.

Shoshi disappeared from our daily life. She was assigned her own room, as if she were an adult. Some kids in the class thought she had probably moved into her parents' apartment. But I didn't. I suspected she'd be terrified of her father's temper. But I didn't want to say it out loud, so I just nodded, regardless of what rumors I heard. Occasionally we'd see her in the kibbutz dining room. She was working in the kitchen. She seemed to force a tired smile when we passed each other. Everyone pretended that everything was just fine. After the baby came, she was assigned to the laundry and clothing warehouse. It was lighter work and you could take breaks more easily than in the kitchen with its pressured schedule.

When she reached sixteen she was instructed, I suspect, though she never said anything, to marry her boyfriend. The kibbutz did not put on the normal wedding celebration and fanfare. In fact, I don't remember a ceremony at all, just the knowledge that they were now married. Around that time, I heard rumors that she had confided in her older sister, when she was seven months pregnant, that "something was wrong." It was too late for an abortion. The kibbutz authorities, probably the nurse and the education committee chairwoman, decided her fate. Her childhood, schooling, and friendships ended in eighth grade. Though her baby was a healthy, chubby, and cheerful boy, she wasn't welcomed by the other new mothers, who were a decade or more her seniors.

She turned eighteen the summer between our eleventh and twelfth grades. She no longer looked like us. She had imperceptibly morphed into the typical appearance and demeanor of the other young mothers on the kibbutz, all in their early twenties. Just a bit thick around the middle, her steps a little heavier, fatigue always lurking in the corners of her eyes. Near the end of that summer her boyfriend (now husband) completed his army service, and they announced their departure from the kibbutz. They were going to a new settlement in the West Bank. There, everyone was starting from scratch, and they wouldn't need to know her exact age.

I ran into her on the sidewalk one afternoon, her three-and-a-half-year-old pulling on her hand. "I want a popsicle, Mommy," he whined.

"Hi," I said softly, "I heard you are leaving."

She just nodded.

"You promised!" the boy insisted.

"Yes, sweetie, in just a few minutes," she said in a more tender, patient tone than I would have expected—certainly more so than the usual one young mothers on the kibbutz employed with whining children. Was it a show for my sake? Or had she become a really good mother—something I hadn't considered, let alone expected?

"I understand, of course," I said, "but how will you manage? You won't have any people there to help you. It will be so hard!"

"Yes . . ." she said, "but not as hard as having a hundred pairs of eyes judging you every single day."

I understood, but my heart sank. Maybe I could have helped her early enough to avoid all of this? I hadn't told anyone what I saw, not even my mother. Maybe I was partially responsible; maybe I had grievously failed her? The kibbutz certainly had.

She had to leave. Eventually, for this and many other reasons, I would leave too.

CHAPTER 18

Jerusalem

We ran into the shelter when the first siren sounded on June 6, 1967, and spent the first two days of the Six-Day War inside, eating, sleeping, and passing the time listening to news reports and biting our nails. By the third day we stayed outside all day, sitting around on folding chairs we had brought from home. You'd think we were at the beach, except the radio was on all the time. We held our breaths as we followed the overwrought, hoarse voices of reporters from the Sinai, the Golan Heights, and, most stirring, from Jerusalem.

"Are we still going to go to America?" I asked my parents three days later, when the war was over. "We'll know in a few days," my father said, "as soon as I can find out when the American Embassy in Tel Aviv will reopen for business. We still have to go there to get our visas."

I had been stunned when my father first announced in April that he had been invited by UNESCO to go to Boston and work with the group of physicists there. They were rewriting all the textbooks for teaching physics in America. My father worked with a sister group at the Weizmann Institute in Rehovot, adapting the American model to Israeli schools. I couldn't believe that my father had been chosen. "The Rehovot Group" was run by one of Israel's most distinguished scientists, Professor Amos De-Shalit, a physicist of international renown. All the other members had master's degrees, if not doctorates. My father had no diplomas. He had studied at the Hebrew University for a total of one year. He got his start in physics as the science teacher at the regional high school. He had worked his way up from carpentry by dint of his ability as an autodidact. "Go to Jerusalem and take as many courses as they'll let you. See how much of the four-year bachelor degree you can cram into one," the kibbutz's Higher Education Committee had instructed my father, "We can only afford to send you to study for one year."

Why was my father picked from among the group of professors with distinguished academic careers? Because he was a carpenter. As the group developed new lesson plans for teaching physics in a "hands-on" manner, my father built all the prototypes of the instru-

My father with one of the instruments that he designed and built for physics experiments.

ments used in lab experiments. The leader of the Boston group, who often came to the Weizmann Institute for consultations, had seen those instruments and thought he could use my father's skills in the "mother ship."

So we were going to America! I was so thrilled that I felt I would burst. I tripled the number of English-for-beginners storybooks I had already been devouring, finishing two a day. We began to talk about what we would pack for a year in Boston. But starting in May, the anxious buildup towards the war took over and made me almost forget about the trip.

Then, more quickly than imaginable, the war was over and we were back to planning our journey. It was only five days after the end of the war when we set out for Tel Aviv to get our visas. My oldest brother was in the army and, in fact, had been in fierce battles in the West Bank. He couldn't come with us, but the army promised that at the end of the year, though his service would not yet be completed, he would be given a month's leave and could join us on our grand tour through Europe that we'd planned for when we returned from the year in America.

It's impossible to recapture the feeling of total security after the victories of the Six-Day War, which made my parents confident about going abroad for a year while their son was still on active duty. They worried about missing him and about his loneliness without the family (he dismissed that—he had many friends, the whole kibbutz was there, and he had a girlfriend), but not about his safety.

My parents, my middle brother, and I—the youngest—boarded the 6:20 a.m. bus at the kibbutz for our three-hour trip to Tel Aviv. The bus was overfull because regular service had been reinstated only the day before. Several kilometers outside of Afula, a nothing town but a central bus hub for Northern Israel, the driver came to a sudden stop on the side of the road. There was neither a settlement there, nor even a rural bus stop. But there was a group of soldiers camped by the roadside.

"Anyone need to go to Tel Aviv? Or anywhere on the way there?" the driver shouted after he opened the door.

Three soldiers, their uniforms dusty and stained, climbed onto the bus, lugging their guns and backpacks. The whole bus broke into loud clapping. People at the front jumped up and invited—no, demanded—the soldiers take their seats. The soldiers waved them off. But the passengers insisted; each soldier must take a double seat so he could spread out in comfort.

"Do it!" the bus driver ordered the soldiers. And they obeyed, clearly embarrassed by all the attention.

"Only for a short while," one soldier said and the other two nodded, as each one slid onto a hard seat. "Then we'll switch."

"Sure," the people who had given up their seats said. But within minutes all three soldiers were asleep, slumped over their heavy packs, their guns pressed against their shoulders. Not one of them woke up during the rest of the drive to Tel Aviv. As the bus emptied at the central bus station, passengers pressed packets of gum, chocolate bars, and cigarette boxes into the soldiers' hands.

The American Embassy was nearly empty. No Israelis were there to request visas for leisure trips to the United States. We felt a tinge of guilt. Leave the country so soon? But we were being sent; my father was on a mission for UNESCO. It was a once-in-a-lifetime opportunity. We got approved on the spot. The consulate official assured us that the visas would be mailed the next day and would reach us well before our departure date.

It was late afternoon when we were done, too late to make it back home. I thought we would stay overnight with our Tel Aviv friends and head back to the kibbutz early the next morning. But when we got up the next day my parents announced that we were going to Jerusalem. I was so excited! I had only been to Jerusalem once, on a class trip in sixth grade. It was a big deal to go there. Even under normal circumstances, it involved a five-hour bus journey from the kibbutz. I was so thrilled about visiting Jerusalem that it didn't occur to me to ask why we were going now. All I thought about at that moment was that we were already well over halfway there.

In fact, it took four hours. One bus after another at the Tel Aviv central bus station filled up with soldiers returning home from the war. The civilians urged all of them to cut in line. Everyone waited very patiently (a rarity for Israelis) until there were free seats and no more soldiers. We arrived in Jerusalem after noon, the sun already frying the city and its inhabitants. From the central bus station we took a city bus to the end of the line, where the border between Israel and Jordan had been just two weeks earlier.

We joined a huge throng of people all walking towards the Tower of David at the entrance to the Old City of Jerusalem. We climbed along a dusty path, the sun beating on our heads. Coming from our scorching-hot kibbutz, we all had hats (it was practically blasphemous to go out without a hat at home), but most of the others were bareheaded, except for the religious ones, men with their skullcaps of various sizes and women in kerchiefs and scarves.

The crowd was enormous and the path narrow. We trudged up slowly and it seemed like it would take hours to reach our destination—the Jaffa Gate and then the Wailing Wall.

I was not a complainer as a rule and prided myself on being tough, but after two hours, when it looked like we were not yet halfway there, I asked my parents: "Why are we doing this now when it's so crowded? Half of the country is here. Wouldn't it make more sense to wait and do it another time?"

My parents both looked at me with great surprise.

"Think about it," my mother said. "In less than two weeks we are going to America. By the time we come back—in a year—it will have been returned to Jordan as part of the peace deal. And then it will be much harder to visit."

"Of course," I said apologetically. "What was I thinking?"

CHAPTER 19

America!

I had to tell myself when I woke up every morning, *Yes, we really are going to America!* When I'd first learned in April that we were going to go to the United States for a year, I did not think of it as "America," but as "A-M-E-R-I-C-A!!!" I had seen *West Side Story* (the film, of course, not the Broadway musical) and couldn't stop humming "I like to be in America." We were going because my father was sent by UNESCO to work in Boston with a group that was revolutionizing the teaching of physics in high school. The Boston group had established a satellite at the Weizmann Institute in Israel where my father went once a week to work with the local team. The project director, Uri Haber-Schaim, shuttled back and forth between Boston and Rehovot. He and his family would be our hosts. I was delighted to learn that he had a daughter, Navah, exactly my age.

Then, in May, came the threat of war, and going to America was pushed to the far edge of my brain, where fantasies resided. During the first two days of the Six-Day War, the whole kibbutz was ordered into the shelters. I was assigned to the one near the toddler house, where, in normal times, I worked the afternoon shift, getting four two-year-olds up from their nap and out of their soiled diapers (cloth, of course, which had to be rinsed in a bucket and put into the huge bin that I would drag on a four-wheeled cart to the central laundry at the end of my shift). This was actually the same shelter I had been taken to as a four-year-old during the 1956 Sinai Campaign. While I did not have any memories of specific facts or events, I had an eerie feeling of déjà vu when I rushed into the dank, cave-like room holding a squirming toddler in my arms.

Mostly we sat in the shelter glued to the radio, but at night everyone crammed onto bunk beds and cots and tried to get some sleep. After three days it was clear we were no longer in danger, and daily life resumed, minus all the kibbutz's young men, who were at various fronts. It was our lucky war—no one from the kibbutz was killed. One member, who fought in Jerusalem, took a bullet through his neck, but miraculously it hit no blood vessels. There was some damage to his vocal cords—he would speak with a slightly hoarse voice from then on, but that's all. A few millimeters over would have meant instant death.

Six days later the war was over, and after a few more days my father got word that his trip to the United States was back on. I don't know what seemed to me more surreal—Israel's lightning-fast victories on three fronts or the Korati family's trip to America. On the way to America we stopped to visit relatives in Bern, Switzerland. We went out each morning to look for the famous vistas of the Alps. Nothing: all we saw were clouds, puffy cotton wool one day, a gray upside-down sea the next. Each day was cloudier than the previous one, and we had not even a glimpse of one mountain. By the third day my brother Eran (three years my senior) and I were frustrated. Our parents had promised us the most spectacular snowy peaks, "better than anything you'd ever seen in a picture," they said. "Really," we complained to them, "from back home in Kfar Ruppin you are able to NOT see the Alps better!"

At our next stop, London, to visit George, my parents' youth movement buddy from Prague (who had volunteered in Mauritius for the

RAF and ended up in British military intelligence), we did experience something unlike anything we had experienced back home. George came to pick us up at Heathrow in a blood-red Triumph two-seater convertible, the hood folded back. We squeezed in: my mother in front, my father in the back, knees awkwardly bent as he pressed in sideways on the narrow ledge intended for luggage. My brother and I perched on the sides above the back wheels, half a bottom's cheek hanging over the edge. Our only protection was the pile of suitcases lashed with rope above the trunk. It was exhilarating. But, when I said to my mother after we arrived safely at George's house, "That you cannot see back home," she blurted out, "And it's a good thing!"

My brother and I used that in our new motto. Everything was categorized as either "We have it at home, and better," or "We don't have it at home, and it's a good thing." Buckingham Palace's Changing of the Guard (such a waste of resources!), double decker buses (imagine the accidents on Israel's crowded, narrow roads), and, of course, a queen. Needless to say, the falafel that George was so proud he could get in London didn't come close to the one at home.

Only two things, besides the ride in the Triumph, that Eran and I saw earned our appreciation (as in "We don't have it at home and it's too bad"): British soccer and, in the US, Howard Johnson's twenty-eight ice cream flavors. At the kibbutz we had chocolate and vanilla after every Friday evening dinner and, once a month, strawberry.

As we settled in at a booth at Howard Johnson's, Eran and I tried to decipher the menu, needing our parents' help with words we did not know: raspberry, blueberry, caramel, and peanut brittle. When my shock wore off, I announced, "We'll have to come here twenty-seven more times to try all the flavors, so in eleven months . . . that means about two and a half times a month, so more often than every other week." My father looked at me with a wide grin. He was just happy I was so good at math. When the waitress came for our order, my world was turned upside down: I learned that you could get a banana split with three flavors, not to mention whipped cream and chocolate syrup and a cherry on top, all in one swoop! It was beyond belief. The only downside was that we could sample all the flavors in just nine visits.

We spent the first month in the United States at Wellesley College, where my father participated in a summer course for physics teachers and my mother reveled in walks in the woods and mushroom hunting. There was a Howard Johnson in town—a half-hour walk from the campus, so Eran and I were happy. In late August we settled in Newton, a well-off Boston neighborhood, because we'd been told the high school there was reputed to be the best public school in America, and my father could walk across the Mass Turnpike to his office in Watertown. Soon after school started, I encountered something even more astounding: all classes were cancelled for the final game of the World Series. Carl Yastrzemski, the Red Sox's golden boy, was to bat first. Yastrzemski was an American hero's name? Didn't it have to be Smith or Jones? And "Red Sox" is a name for a storied baseball team? Not Cougars, Giants, Chieftains, or something like that? If sox were worthy to be a team's mascot, were there "White Sox," "Blue Sox" "Orange?" Indeed, there were, I was flabbergasted to learn.

Our homeroom teacher, Mr. Rosenberg, announced that the whole school would assemble in the auditorium and watch the game on the school's two twenty-eight-inch black and white TV sets. Pandemonium broke out in the classroom, and everyone quickly gathered their things, stuffed them into their book bags, and rushed out. I approached the teacher's desk when the classroom emptied and politely asked if I could go home instead. Mr. Rosenberg looked at me with a furrowed brow; then his forehead smoothed and he smiled. "Ah, yes, of course. I know we don't have baseball in Israel. So sure, you don't have to stay." I had no idea why he said "we." At the time it hadn't dawned on me that he was Jewish, despite his name.

I walked home through nearly empty streets. I passed the neighborhood coffee shop, which was crammed with people watching the game. Sounds of the announcer's voice rising and falling with each hit floated out of many of the houses I passed. I overheard some score calls for the Red Sox and some for the Cardinals. The latter seemed even crazier than "sox": there was a team of Catholic clergy? Well, clearly, baseball was something of a religion here, and that's why school was cancelled and everyone but me was in front of a TV or radio. Did the Cardinals' fans kneel as they watched?

It was rather eerie walking the seemingly deserted town. I kept my mind from wandering towards anxiety by collecting bright red, orange, and yellow fall leaves. I was bewitched by the vibrant colors and had to add the fall foliage to my short list of things that were better in America. But this baseball phenomenon was certainly an item to add to the list that Eran and I kept of "We don't have it in Israel and it's a good thing we don't."

* * *

Thanksgiving was approaching. Eran was working as a chauffeur-chaperone-handyman for an elderly lady in the neighborhood. She informed him on his first day: "I am what they call a 'blue blood.' My ancestors came on the Mayflower." Needless to say, he didn't know what either term meant. My mother explained it and concluded by reciting, with a hint of contempt, the famous toast:

> And this is good old Boston,
> The home of the bean and the cod.
> Where the Lowells talk only to Cabots,
> And the Cabots talk only to God.

"Mrs. Mayflower," as we called her in our house, was a bit smitten with my brother, who was a strikingly handsome eighteen-year-old. So she not only paid him well; she also sold him her 1946 dual-shade-green Pontiac Streamliner, with less than 20,000 miles, for twenty-five dollars. Her only condition was that he drive her wherever and whenever she wanted. He was thrilled—he loved driving and never imagined he'd own a car.

It was in this car that Eran drove Mrs. Mayflower and our family to have Thanksgiving dinner at the Sturbridge Inn, on the outskirts of historic Sturbridge Village. She insisted on giving us "the true Thanksgiving experience": a candle-lit dinner in the old white clapboard colonial building. When she first extended the invitation she had given Eran a postcard to take home and show us: two red doors on either end, a four-arch colonnade between them, and a second story pointed-roof tower in the middle.

"It looks like a church to me," I said.

"The story of the Pilgrims is kind of a religion here," my mother said and explained further that the story had been preserved in Old Sturbridge Village. "We'll take a trip there in spring to see the whole place."

It snowed the whole way to the inn, and by the time we arrived after a grueling three-hour drive, everything—houses, trees, and cars—was draped in two feet of snow. It was not the first time I had seen snow; earlier in the fall there had been two snowfalls, which enchanted me. But now I understood that those had been just a preview, a mere few inches. This was a *blanket* of snow. It was breathtaking.

The candle-lit dinner was beautiful, and I kept looking at the windows where the flames' reflection danced against the background of a snow quilt covering the hedge outside. The food itself, served on lavishly piled pewter platters, was strange to us. We had never had a whole roasted turkey and didn't know what "stuffing" was. We were used to turkey meat in Israel, where it's used as a stand-in for beef. Pairing turkey with the overly sweet cranberry sauce seemed bizarre, and why would you make a pie out of a vegetable instead of cherries or strawberries?

Stuffed to near explosion, we drove all the way back. Finally home well after midnight, Eran and I hardly needed to say it " . . . don't . . . and it's a good thing."

A week after this immersion in American culture, on the first Monday in December, I went to school and suddenly understood everything that was said. Imperceptibly, I had grown accustomed to Bostonian speech and the social codes of high school. I even went to a football game. I found the rules of the game incomprehensible and the cheerleaders' gymnastics baffling, another " . . . don't . . . and it's a good thing." But I did relate to the esprit-de-corps of my classmates. I shot up with them and stomped my feet on bleachers for every few yards' advancement of the ball. I even bought a dress with orange and black stripes—the school colors—and wore it to the games. It fit a bit too tightly but I flaunted it nevertheless.

I gradually let go of the post–Six-Day War euphoria of Israel and turned my attention to the cauldron of the civil rights movement in America. Its call for equality and a utopian society connected seamlessly to my kibbutznik's idealism. Newton High School, I now learned, was a hotbed of activism. I was invited to join a group that worked on neighborhood desegregation— a totally novel concept. Tom, the key organizer, had a crew cut so I assumed he was an all-American boy. Just before Christmas, people in the group talked about their holiday plans. When I asked if he was excited about Christmas, he answered, "Of course not. I'm Jewish."

"You are Jewish?" I exclaimed in disbelief.

"Of course," he answered with a shrug. "Most of us in the group are. Except, thankfully, the two blacks we have. That makes us more kosher; you know what I mean . . ."

I nodded a "yes," while actually stunned that he used the word "kosher."

Tom and his friends schooled me in the history of racism and the subtleties of housing segregation. I kept saying to myself—and occasionally to them—"We don't have it in Israel, and it's a good thing." I was so very naïve, having been sheltered in my kibbutz cocoon. I had never seen the poor neighborhoods of Mizrahi Jews in Israel's cities. I had never visited the bleak housing projects in development towns housing North African Jews. Even when in Beit She'an, the town only a few miles from my kibbutz, I was blind to the poverty. In fact, social unrest about systemic discrimination was already brewing in those neighborhoods and would burst into violent protests by the Black Panthers movement in Israel (influenced by the American movement) in 1971. When members of the group spoke of what today we call "income inequality," I explained how egalitarian Israeli society was in general and touted the "pure" equality of the kibbutz. I knew almost nothing about the poor in Israel. When they debated flag burnings in protest against the Vietnam War, I only listened. When they asked my opinion, I said: "Maybe that's the way to do it in America, but we would never do that in Israel."

In the course of the year, Navah and I became close friends, and in the spring she invited me for a week at the Putney School in Vermont, a boarding school where she had started as a student in September. She assured me I would love it, as I would go to all her classes and activities with her. "But," she said, "you can't just come. You have to do something for the school when you are here." I thought about it for a moment: "I'll give a talk about the kibbutz."

"Great idea!" Navah said. She was sure the topic would interest her schoolmates. But she cautioned me that, once the date was set, I had better be well prepared.

"You will give your talk at our Sunday evening all-school gathering. It's almost sacred here. The week before you Bobby Kennedy is speaking,"

"Bobby Kennedy as in Robert Kennedy? Are you kidding me?"

"Yes, the very one. His daughter is a student here."

"I can't believe it!" I said. "Don't worry," I assured her, "I'll write it out and practice my delivery with my parents."

In early April I took the bus to Keene, New Hampshire, and a shuttle from there to the Putney School. I hoped to God I had gotten off at the right spot in Keene and on to the correct shuttle van. When I arrived, I told Navah it had been easy. I spent the whole week with her going to all her classes and to her work assignment in the school's dairy farm. It all seemed rather like home—most of all the meals were in the communal dining room—so I felt a little less nervous about explaining what a kibbutz was to the students. I met Kathleen

Kennedy and mentioned my upcoming talk, being careful, as Navah had instructed me, not to make a big deal of her name and her dad. She assured me the students would be very interested in my stories. "Don't worry about your talk," she assured me. "Everyone will listen carefully. They did so pretty well when my dad spoke last week."

Sunday evening came. I had not been able to get anything down at dinner, so just sipped some tea with lemon to warm my throat. It felt like a big rock was stuck in it, constricting the flow of words. But as I began to speak, my throat slowly opened up and the words flowed out, as if of their own accord. And the students listened, indeed very attentively, and then had a lot of questions. They saw many similarities to their school.

"We have a farm where we work every day," one student said.

"Yes," I said politely. "I took a tour. It's very nice. But ours at the kibbutz is about a hundred times bigger."

"Our dorms sound very much like your children's house," another student piped up.

I smiled.

"Yes, but ours start the day a baby comes home from the hospital."

And so it went with Putney School, at least in my eyes, falling short of my kibbutz in Israel on every count.

Several students came up to me afterwards and congratulated me on my talk. A couple even said it was more interesting than Bobby Kennedy's the week before. "We knew what he would say, but this, what you talked about, I've never heard of before."

"Well," I demurred, "I wouldn't . . ." and left the half sentence hanging.

When I got home I told my parents and all my school friends about it. In the telling, the fact that I had spoken one week after Bobby Kennedy became the highlight of the whole trip. I started following his election campaign closely and almost envying Tom and the rest of my "civil rights friends" at Newton High who were planning to work on his campaign over the summer. I was now proud of the Boston accent I was slowly acquiring.

On June fifth, just before heading to school I turned on the TV for the morning news. I wanted to see if there was going to be a report on the one-year anniversary of the Six-Day War. Mayhem. It took several minutes to comprehend the reporting: Bobby Kennedy had been shot. My Bobby Kennedy!

I stared at the TV, surprised to find tears in my eyes. I told my parents I couldn't go to school; I had to keep watching. They agreed right away. I didn't ask why. Were they worried there would be a student walkout, maybe even a riot? We had watched with horror the coverage of Martin Luther King's assassination only two months earlier and the riots that ensued. It would have been in bad taste to say, "That couldn't happen in Israel," so no one had said it out loud, but I had certainly said it to myself. Little did we know. No one could have imagined then the assassination of Yitzhak Rabin in 1995.

I watched non-stop. The next day, when the report of Kennedy's death came, I was stunned. I instinctively stood up at attention, to show my respect. Next a commercial came on—whatever inane jingle had been slotted before. I threw my shoe at the TV. How dare they show such utter disrespect for *my* Bobby Kennedy?

CHAPTER 20

Going Home

My big suitcase was packed so full that my brother and I had to sit on it in order to zip it shut. My second piece of luggage was my pride and joy: a record player. I had saved all my baby-sitting money all year. The going rate for a high school girl in our upscale neighborhood was $1.25 an hour. Babysitting two or three times a month allowed me to buy a record player, built into a hard case, and several LP's. The records I chose would almost be contraband when I got back to the kibbutz: The Beatles' *Revolver*, *Hard Day's Night*, and *Magical Mystery Tour*; Simon and Garfunkel's *Sounds of Silence* and *Hair*. I also bought one classical music record: Mozart's *Eine Kleine Nachtmusik*, both trying to impress my classmates and genuinely loving the piece.

I was especially eager to play *Hair* for my classmates because I had actually seen it live in New York. My parents, who aspired much more than I had realized at the time to be not just cosmopolitan but also hip, took us to see it on Broadway. They probably trimmed the grocery-shopping list by a third for several months to afford the tickets, though I didn't notice anything. I ogled the magnificent Afros.

My breath froze in my windpipe when several actors walked on stage stark naked.

Much of the libretto went right over my head. I certainly didn't know what "sodomy," "fellatio," and "pederasty" meant and didn't, therefore, fully understand the next line: "Father, why do these words sound so nasty?" But, oh, I was so worldly and cool! What will they say back at my Beit Yeladim when I describe the show, play by play? I kept the program to add visuals. I couldn't wait to see my classmates' faces when I told them about the nudity.

The year had been mind-blowing (that expression itself a part of the mental explosion). While my heart had been homesick for the kibbutz all year, my head was filled with startling new impressions and ideas: the struggle for civil rights, the assassinations of Martin Luther King and Bobby Kennedy, the demonstrations against the Vietnam War, and the student uprising in Europe. At the beginning of May my brother had gone off to Paris "to see what they're up to there." The riots of May 1968 were turning the cobblestones of Paris streets—and many other French towns—to ammunition depots, as students hurled them at police. Everyone claimed to have spotted Danny the Red. "I'll find him," Eran assured us with his accustomed swagger. When we met him in July in London he was wearing a shirt with no buttons and one flip-flop. "A policemen chased me in Paris," he explained nonchalantly, "grabbed my collar from behind. All the buttons flew off. I got away and ran. I suppose he has the buttons and one flip-flop."

Still, I couldn't wait to go home to the kibbutz, my class, Friday night dinners and dancing at the chadar ochel, the swimming pool, and the open fields. The list ran through my head like the paper roll printout of an adding machine. But I also didn't want to miss all the exciting events on the horizon in America: the "Poor People's Campaign" that Tom and his friends were working on with a rally planned for the National Mall, the two parties' national conventions, and the Apollo mission that the science nerds in my AP math class were constantly chattering about. The most titillating question was: will there be a second Summer of Love?

My large suitcase had all the things I was bringing back home. There was still a medium-size pile of items I couldn't just discard. Taking another suitcase would be too cumbersome: I only have two hands. What to do with those semi-cherished items seemed like an insurmountable dilemma. I thought sleeping on it might help. That night I had a dream that threw me for a loop. In the dream I arrive at the Beit Yeladim with all my luggage. My classmates gather around me and eagerly eye my things. Suddenly they pounce on the large suitcase, unzipping it, taking items out and showing each other, trying my clothes on, opening packets, examining my toiletries. Next they unclasp the record player case and pull out the cord to plug into the wall socket. I am flabbergasted and helpless. All I can do is beseech them, repeating, "That's not the way we do it in America," over and over.

I woke up with the dream still vivid in my eyes. I was terribly distraught. How could I say "the way WE do it in AMERICA?" How could I distance myself from my classmates, my home? I asked my mother, who had spent the year in Boston training as a psychotherapist, "What does it mean that I said that in the dream?"

I got a thumbnail sketch of Freud's *The Interpretation of Dreams* infused with my mother's reassuring voice. Yes, the year in America had changed me; there were new things I was bringing to my class on the kibbutz; they were valuable—new understanding, bigger perspectives, and fresh lessons. But I need not worry about going back, my mother told me. No doubt my classmates would be more than excited to learn about American ways. And no doubt I would fit right in, back to the warm cocoon of my childhood.

It turned out to be one of the very few times in my life when my mother was wrong. "That's the way we do it in America" stuck with me. The suitcase I had brought back was never fully emptied and put away. I carried new notions and perspectives with me, and, though I never said it to my friends, I now felt an outsider in my own home. I began to fantasize about one day going back, maybe to university. I had seen Harvard Yard. It left an indelible impression, refreshed when *Love Story* came out in 1970.

After our year in America I couldn't find my place back in our small local school. "That's the way we do it in America"—from my dream back in Newton—meant I was way ahead of my class in math, science, and, of course, English. I replaced those classes with independent study to make up the material I had missed in Bible, Hebrew grammar, and geography of Israel. I was all caught up to my classmates after two months, and now I was bored. Our school was so small that there was no eleventh grade, so there was no class for me to advance into. I was becoming a real nuisance, constantly challenging the teachers with counter arguments and impossible questions.

I needed to go to a larger school. My parents investigated several options and suggested Beit Yerach, the Jordan Valley regional kibbutz high school on the banks of the Sea of Galilee. When I visited and sat in on classes, I was sold. The teachers were excellent and the principal, thoughtful and charismatic. The rich curriculum and extensive campus with sprawling green lawns beckoned me. I could live at nearby Kibbutz Afikim during the week, "adopted" by the family of a woman who grew up in Kfar Ruppin. I would come home for weekends.

My parents shielded me from the fact that the principal of our local school had tried to dissuade them and prevent my transfer. "How could you," he'd said to my father who'd been the physics teacher there for many years, "you of all people, disparage the school by removing your daughter? You realize the damage to us? You would be announcing to one and all that the school is not good enough." How, he pressed further, could my parents put my individual needs ahead of the collective good?

Beit Yerach was a much larger and academically more rigorous school. I flourished there. When I came home for the weekends I no longer felt an easy rapport with my classmates. I drifted away from all but one of them, Rafi, the other outsider in the group. He was struggling to find his own path as he became aware of his homosexuality. Of course, it was something he never spoke about out loud. We became good friends, two odd peas in that very long collective pod.

CHAPTER 21

What God Wants You to Do

I admitted to myself, but not to my mother, that my stomach was in knots on the bus ride from our kibbutz to my high school, Beit Yerach, by the southern tip of the Kineret.

"Don't worry too much," I told her. "I go early in the morning and there has never been shelling at that time. They are probably still asleep over there in Jordan, at that hour."

As a matter of fact, the roughly twenty-mile bus ride between my kibbutz and my new school traversed the "battlefield" where nearly every day the PLO (Palestine Liberation Organization) fighters peppered the kibbutzim with mortar shells from across the Jordan River, usually in the evening. My mother was understandably worried, while I, a cocky teenager, never thought to worry about her. She too rode that bus every Sunday for her work in the Jordan Valley Family Therapy Clinic.

As a regular on the bus route, she usually picked the seat right by the front door. She loved to watch the scenery change with the seasons, especially as the gray-brown landscape surrendered to resplendent green after the first winter rains. On one of those weekly rides, after passing Kibbutz Gesher, which is just past the journey's midpoint, she caught a shrieking sound whizzing over the bus. She knew the sound from frequent shelling at home and instinctively ducked. An instant later a loud explosion rocked the bus. The driver almost lost his grip on the wheel and the bus swerved to the far side of the road. Luckily, there was no oncoming traffic.

"Stop!" yelled some of the passengers.

"No, go faster!" screamed others.

The driver was befuddled but managed to right the bus back into its lane.

"Stop right there!" my mother ordered the driver and pointed to where a large drainage tunnel ran under the road into a deep ditch alongside the asphalt. He hit the breaks.

"Everyone out of the bus!" my mother called out. "Duck and crawl down the aisle to the door. Keep order! At the door, jump off the bus and into that culvert."

Everyone obeyed, as if she were an IDF general. They all squeezed into the culvert and ditch, which was still muddy from the last rain. A middle-aged woman with a kerchief tightly bound around her head stood up and began to pray, calling out to God to save her.

"Get down!" said my mother, pulling on her sleeve.

"I have to pray! God will listen . . . God just wants us to pray to be saved."

"Yes," my mother, a lifelong atheist, said, "but God also wants you to help Him save you by lying down in the ditch."

The woman looked at her husband, crouching nearby, his distinguished rabbinical beard smudged by the muddy ground. He nodded. She got down on her hands and knees as two more shells whistled above them and exploded on the hillside across the road. She wasn't the only one praying.

Soon, IDF artillery responded with a massive volley of shells. Minutes later two IDF jeeps and, right after them, an armored personnel carrier arrived with the regional commander at the helm. They surveyed the crowd of passengers huddled in the culvert and ditch and praised the bus driver for his quick and appropriate response. He didn't correct them. He would probably receive a citation for courage under fire from the Egged bus company.

The IDF commander instructed the passengers to get back on the bus to continue on the drive to Tiberias with the army vehicles' escort. My mother took her seat up front and chatted up the still-shaken driver to ease his nerves. When she got up to get off at her stop the whole bus burst into applause. She waved farewell and regally descended the stairs.

About a month later there was a knock on her door at 3:00 p.m. in the afternoon. She knew it must be either an urgent matter or a visitor; no kibbutznik would come to your door during the 2:00 p.m. to 4:00 p.m. *Schlafstunde* (afternoon nap—almost sacred on the kibbutz). She opened the door to find a very religious family: a man with a flowing white beard, a middle-aged woman with a headscarf wound tightly around her scalp, an elderly grandmother with an embroidered kerchief tied under double chin, and two girls in ankle-length skirts.

"Come in," she said, not sure who they were, though they did look vaguely familiar.

"We are from the bus," said the man.

"The bus?"

"Yes, the bus to Tiberias when you saved us; in the shelling near Gesher."

"Oh, yes, of course," my mother said, "when I told you that you needed to help God."

The middle-aged woman nodded and smiled shyly.

"I didn't mean to offend you," my mother said. "It was . . . an emergency."

"You said exactly the right thing," the woman said. "Even my husband—he is a rabbi—said so."

My mother relaxed in relief and invited them to sit and rest while she got some refreshments. She pointed out where the bathroom was. Kfar Ruppin being at the end of the road, the bus ride to get there was always long. One needed a clean restroom at the end of it, as the hygiene of restrooms at the central bus station was unacceptable. They thanked her warmly and lined up.

By the time they were done my mother had set a platter of sliced coffee cake with dried fruit pieces and glasses of tea, with lemon slices on the side. She handed each of them a plate with a piece of cake. The two girls immediately took a bite, but the older women held the cake at a distance. When my mother added, "Home-made English tea cake. My best recipe!" they all immediately put their plates down and tensed their shoulders.

"Nisht Kosher," they whispered to each other, then repeated more loudly, and apologetically, to my mother, "It's not kosher." (No kitchens, neither the big communal one nor the tiny ones in members' homes, were kosher.)

"It is," the husband spoke up. "In the home if this great lady, everything is kosher."

CHAPTER 22

Under the Bed, Below Sea Level

"Under the bed," my husband, David, and I have been saying for nearly five decades when people ask us how we met. "And 238 meters below sea level," I add if they seem sufficiently intrigued to want the full story.

It was in the summer of 1970. I had just graduated from high school and was spending the summer at home on the kibbutz preparing for the matriculation exams. My friend Navah asked if a pal she had just met at the advanced Hebrew class at Ulpan Akiva in Netanyah could tag along with her. She was coming to our kibbutz and to be with us while waiting a few weeks before her IDF draft. The year we lived in Newton my father had worked with her father in physics curriculum development; her mother and mine got very close, and Navah and I had become good friends.

After I returned to the kibbutz, Navah and I had corresponded for a couple of years until she graduated from high school and decided to come to Israel to serve in the army. She had dual citizenship, and those were the days when service in the IDF seemed glamorous and patriotic. We were not fully cognizant yet of the way the Occupation of the West Bank and Gaza entrenched the army and all of Israeli society in a nightmare that has not yet ended.

"This David," Navah said on the phone, "is really into Jewish things. You'll have a lot to talk about. And his Hebrew is great, so he can work anywhere on the kibbutz where he's needed." There was something in her voice. I had a hunch she liked him—yes, that way. Which primed me for romantic possibilities, too. It didn't take much at that age.

And he, I gathered, was also looking for romance—but more along the lines of Hemingway battlefield allure. My kibbutz was then in the midst of a period of almost nightly shelling by the PLO from across the Jordan River. I had to make sure Navah and this David were prepared.

"You both realize," I said, "that we have to run to the shelters almost every evening."

"We know," she said.

"But don't worry too much," I injected. "It usually only lasts about twenty minutes. They lob three or four mortar shells at us. We run to the shelters, the IDF pounds them with heavy artillery, and soon we get the 'All clear' and can leave the shelters."

By summer 1970 my classmates and I were mostly inured to the actual danger. The mini-war of attrition had been going on since the beginning of 1968. It was rote by now. The fact that a year earlier two teenagers had been killed by mortar shell fragments as they ran to the shelter had somewhat faded from memory. They were not kibbutz kids, but rather members of a youth group that had come to the kibbutz for a year. After it happened the whole group left, going back to the safety of their homes in Jerusalem. The kibbutz mourned, and many older members began sleeping in the shelters every night. But life went on.

I had learned of the shelling first from my classmates' letters when I was in Newton. The first few months were terrifying. There were only three shelters in the whole kibbutz, built originally for the 1948 War of Independence. They had been hastily cleaned up and

Top, the children's sleeping quarters in the shelter. Courtesy of Kibbutz Kfar Ruppin's archive. *Bottom,* a photograph of a classmate and myself posing in the shelter for a newspaper story.

used, but for just a few days, during the 1956 Sinai Campaign and again in the Six-Day War. The kibbutz was now crisscrossed with ditches, each about three feet deep, in which you could try to run to a shelter when shells began exploding, or at least crouch and wait it out, safe as long as nothing landed on top of your head.

By the time my family and I returned in the summer of 1968 there were several new shelters. All the children's houses had foot-thick concrete wall passageways that led directly to shelters, and a routine had developed. Young children slept in the shelters every night. We teenagers would gather on the lawn in front of our Beit Yeladim to gossip and await the first whistle of a shell flying overhead. When it came, we ran through the building and passageway into the nearby shelter.

All of this I had relayed to Navah, first in the year in Newton and then in letters. So she was sure she knew what to expect. Explaining it to David was her responsibility. And so they arrived, on August 3, ten days shy of my eighteenth birthday. I was studying for the matriculation exams and preparing to go, come September, to work for a year as a youth movement counselor—a year of service before going into the army.

Navah would share my room, and David settled in with another volunteer in the now-decommissioned baby house. It sat on the eastern slope of "The Hill," where the kibbutz was first established in 1938, a small cluster of buildings at the foot of a watchtower. With an easterly exposure, it was the spot on the kibbutz most vulnerable to shells flying in from across the river. The babies had been moved to a new building in the center of the kibbutz right after the shelling started. Instead, it now housed temporary workers and volunteers.

Navah was exactly as I remembered her from three years earlier. David was as I'd imagined an activist Jewish student from Berkeley would be: big Afro (not quite up to *Hair* standards), scuffed jeans, and John Lennon round-rim glasses. But when I saw him the next morning ready to go out to work in the fields, I had a big surprise: he was wearing a classic old-time kibbutz "Kova Temble" (literally, dunce hat)—a cloth hat with a round brim that hardly anyone on the kibbutz would still be caught in. It turned out it was handmade by his relative at Mishmar Ha-Emek, a storied Ha-Shomer Ha-Tza'ir kibbutz in the Jezreel Valley, where everyone called it "Kova Shifra" in homage to her. He cherished it and didn't seem to mind the amused looks from the young locals passing him on the kibbutz paths.

We spent breakfast and lunch together in the kibbutz chadar ochel every day, discussing twentieth-century Jewish existentialist philosophers Buber and Rosenzweig—the shining lights of the Jewish Revival of the '60s and '70's (both in the US and Israel) and A. D. Gordon's "religion of labor," which animated the Zionist dreams of the chalutzim (pioneers). After work and the requisite afternoon siesta, David, Navah, and I hung out at my parents' house. More talk of Buber, et al. On the third evening after their arrival, we were again engrossed in discussion. My parents were not there; they were out at kibbutz committee meetings of some sort. It was just the three of us.

Somewhere between talk of what constitutes Jewish identity in Israel versus in the US, we heard a piercing whistle right over the house. Then an explosion so loud that I jumped, even though I knew to expect a loud boom immediately after the whistle. "Under the bed," I commanded, taking charge as the local expert. All three of us dove under the bed in the living room—it served as a couch in daytime. We wriggled around in order to fit all essential body parts under the single bed.

"That was too close for us to run to the shelter," I explained as we tried to catch our breath on the cold tile floor. "It's too dangerous to run outside, around the house to the shelter."

They stared at me, clearly unable to say a word.

"We should be fine here," I said cheerily, trying to lift their spirits, "that is, as long as there isn't a direct hit on the house."

I had to be accurate.

"There," I said, "that's the kibbutz siren again. But we don't really need it, do we?" Navah and David remained silent. I tried to pick up the conversation where we'd left off, while two more whistles and explosions shook the house. It wasn't working. I switched to jokes. That wasn't terribly successful either, but, thankfully, now the explosions seemed farther away. Soon we heard distant rumblings.

Roof damage from a mortar shelling of a kibbutz building.
Courtesy of Kibbutz Kfar Ruppin's archive.

"Ah, that's good," I said. "That's the IDF shelling them back. This will be over soon."

Indeed, about ten minutes later we heard the kibbutz siren again, this time signaling the "All clear." Soon it was bedtime. Navah and I went to my room and David went to his. I don't believe he slept at all that night.

The next morning, in daylight, we saw the two-foot hole where the first mortar shell hit, ironically right under an olive tree. It was about twenty feet in front of the house. Broken olive branches were scattered all around, as if a wild animal had demolished half the tree overnight. We found the shell's tail nearby. (My mother saved it for the rest of her life and now it is my son's.) We also saw at least a dozen holes in the front wall of the house, made by the mortar shell's fragments. Had we run out we would have been in their paths.

Nearly three years later and with over three hundred letters between us, David and I married. We've been together, on top of the bed, ever since.

CHAPTER 23

A Real Character

C zech was a real character; everyone agreed about that. He was also a war hero. All of us kids believed it and worshipped him for that. No one else on the kibbutz had been in the Palmach (the elite force of the Haganah, predecessor of the Israel Defense Forces), let alone fought in its battles. Czech was a few years younger than our parents, and, thus, when he arrived in Palestine, he joined the underground militia. Our fathers were "merely" stationed at the kibbutz to defend it from rare attacks in the years leading up to 1948 and, in case of a battle—one that never materialized during the War of Independence.

As far as we were concerned, Czech was responsible for blowing up at least three of the eight bridges the Haganah blew up on "The Night of the Bridges" in 1946; he paved the Burma Road opening the passage to Jerusalem, and was the one who gave Captain Avraham Adan ("Bren") the initial push up the flagpole marking the conquest of Eilat and the end of the War of Independence, on May 15, 1948.

But, as we grew into teenagers, we began to catch stealth exchanges of raised eyebrows or sly winks between adults when we spoke reverentially about Czech's Palmach days. More and more, we came to doubt the stories of his amazing adventures (those same skeptical adults called them *"kuntzim"*—shenanigans), his battlefield heroics, and the injury in combat, which led to his limp.

That limp was his glory, a wound received in a fierce battle in the Negev during the War of Independence. As young children we revered it and blended it with his other unique physical feature: the ability to balance heavy packages on his head and walk along the paths of the kibbutz, hands free. That, we whispered to each other, he learned from the Palestinian women he had observed closely when, as a Palmach operative, he spied on Arab war preparations. We had no factual information to back these rumors, just our ears' and hearts' hunger for heroic tales. But this story fell victim to our jaded teenage commentary: the leg injury was from no great battle, only a car accident; the jeep he was riding ran into a ditch; balancing things on his head was just a "kuntz"—a trick to get attention, first from fellow kibbutz members, later only from visitors.

Still, the tales—perhaps tall tales—kept coming. The first "Czech story" I heard in real time was in 1963. It was during the first Susiyada—National Horse Races—in the nothing town of Afula. There were only three reasons to go to Afula: to change buses at the central station on your way to a real city (Haifa or Tel Aviv), for check-ups (or worse) at the hospital, and to buy Migdan roasted sunflower seeds, widely acknowledged to be the best in the country (even in Haifa and Tel Aviv). The horse race was someone's brainchild for putting Afula on the map. And it made sense; after all, Afula sat in the heart of the Jezreel Valley, surrounded by kibbutzim and *moshavim* (agricultural communal settlements) that, presumably, raised and raced horses.

The kibbutz organized our one GMC lorry, a few small pick-ups and several tractors with wagons to ferry people to the race grounds in open fields on Afula's edge, about an hour's drive (in those days on narrow rough roads; today it takes twenty minutes). We arrived hot and sweaty to find the only seats provided were bales of hay, sure to poke into our bare legs. We all, of course, wore the shorts of the day:

gathered with elastic right below the edge of our buns. Not that it mattered—the bales were all occupied by the time we got there. We'd have to stand the whole time. No one knew how long the races would go on.

So we stood. But not Czech. He was not able to stand for that long because of that injured leg from the Palmach. Within a few minutes of our arrival he disappeared for a while. He returned with a white folding chair, plunked it down in the front row, and sat like a king for the duration. After the races were over he took the chair back to the café from where he had lifted it a few hours earlier. "Someone," he told the owner, "stole one of your chairs. I saw it and recognized it immediately, since I've been to your café several times. I brought it back for you." The café owner gushed with thanks and Czech was invited, from that day forward, to get free coffee and pastry whenever he came by.

It was like that everywhere Czech went—he always had a special deal. And he liked to make deals for others, too. You'd see someone on the kibbutz with an item no one else had, and you'd ask where she or he had bought it. "What store?" they would say, "No store! *Zeh mi-Czech* (it's from Czech). "Zeh mi-Czech" became our standard expression for anything acquired under questionable circumstances. And if you were doing something you shouldn't have, you'd be chided with "Czech said it's OK?"

I thought the Czech Mystique was about to fully burst when I was with him on a delegation from our kibbutz, touring American Jewish communities to raise funds for the UJA (United Jewish Appeal). It was 1971 and the PLO had shelled our kibbutz for over two years. Three or four rockets—on a good night—were launched from the Jordanian side of the border nearly every evening. Four kibbutzniks were chosen—my mother and me (I was fluent in English after a year in the US in 1967–68); Czech (the war hero); and Uri, a boy a year my junior whose good Sabra looks made up for a very rudimentary vocabulary—to tell our tales and raise the bucks.

We arrived in Los Angeles towards the end of our trip. It was the

Kibbutz members at a United Jewish Appeal fundraising
dinner in New York. Senator Jacob Javits is in the center
with Czech on his right. My mother and I are on Javits's left.

jewel in the crown of our tour: we were speaking at a huge dinner
with over five hundred attendees and featuring Yitzhak Rabin (then
Israel's ambassador to the US) as the keynote speaker. Czech was
beaming—he knew Rabin from his days in the Palmach! They were
buddies and had served together on any number of operations. He
made it sound like they shared a tent, if not a mess kit and sleeping
bag.

"Really?" Uri and I feigned innocent disbelief while poking each
other behind Czech's back.

We sat in a cavernous room, filled with fifty round tables. The
kitchen staff worked on covering them with gleaming white table-
cloths and adorning each with ten place settings and water pitchers.
We were waiting for the local organizers to come and give us the
rundown on the evening, probably unnecessary by now, as we had
been drilled in a dozen prior gala dinners: We each sit at a given table
for fifteen minutes and answer questions about what it's like to live
under repeated shellings, then smile, rise quickly, and move to the

adjacent table; repeat story, smile, rise, move on. We each had a zone with six tables to cover in the course of the evening.

We had already seen how our tales of daily danger but determined spirits loosened the purse strings. When it came for the public pledges at the end of each evening, many of those who stood up to announce an increase in their annual donation gave us a knowing wink or broad smile. Our host went over the plan and we nodded and assured her we were well trained. "You'll get your dinner soon, well before the evening's guests arrive. With the table-hopping, you won't have a chance to eat when dinner is served."

Our dinners having been swallowed quickly, our host glanced at her watch and gave us the news that we'd been eagerly awaiting: "Rabin will be here in ten minutes. You'll meet him and introduce yourselves very briefly: name, age, your job on the kibbutz, or your grade in school. He might want to mention you in his speech."

"I won't need to introduce myself," Czech said, with a smile so broad it was as if he were announcing he'd been to the top of Everest.

The host shot him a puzzled frown.

"We know each other. From the Palmach."

"You think he'll remember you?" the host said, and Uri and I echoed with a scoff, "Yes, Czech, are you sure?"

"Prepare yourself that he might not," my mother said, trying, I think, to protect him.

"He'll remember."

"*Nichyeh ve-nir'eh*," I said—"let's see if we live until that moment . . . and then we'll see." At eighteen and a half, I was pretty cocky.

"Say, Czech," said Uri, jumping on my bandwagon, "when you were in the Palmach, had they already discovered electricity?"

"What about the wheel?" I egged us on.

My mother gave me that look of hers—used very sparingly—that made me ashamed of myself.

Before I had a chance to gesture to Uri to zip it, the door clear across the huge room creaked open. A diminutive woman in a tight fitting, tailored suit stepped in. Behind her was Rabin, towering over her, his white shirt tucked in sloppily, jacket slung over his shoulder, no tie. He took two long steps, punctuated on the double by his escort's high heels.

"Czech! What are you doing here?" he called out across the wide expanse of the room and rushed over to clamp his hand over Czech's shoulder. Czech seemed as dumb struck as we were. An unusually short man, Czech had to crane his neck and look up to meet Rabin's eyes. You couldn't help but assign great admiration to that upward gaze.

"Nu, time flies, hah?" Rabin broke the awkward silence. Then, as if he knew to put us—I mean my whole generation—in our place, he added, "How's that leg injury from the battle in the Negev? Still bothering you?"

CHAPTER 24

Never Turn Around

"Never turn around!" I shouted along with the other commanders. "Whatever happens, don't turn around! If you have a problem, put your gun down on the ground, raise your hand and stay facing forward."

"Let me hear you say, Yes!'" we ordered.

"*Ken, ha-mefakedet*—Yes, Commander," the twelve female soldiers, prostrate on their stomachs on the sandy ground in front of us, responded in unison.

All of us non-commissioned officers had been told the story, probably apocryphal, of a soldier at that very shooting range whose rifle had stopped firing. She turned and called out to her commander: "It's not working!" as she squeezed the trigger to demonstrate that the rifle had frozen. She shot her commander in the abdomen.

It was winter 1972, and by far the scariest moment of my army service was overseeing new recruits, four weeks into their six-week basic training, using live fire. Twelve girls at a time (at seventeen and eighteen at that time and place, they were definitely girls, not young women) stretched out on the ground, their rifles aimed at human silhouette targets fifty yards away. We were three NCOs, each one responsible for four of the girls from the unit she commanded. Supervising us was the company officer, who was probably just as terrified.

I had gone into the army after graduation from high school and a year of work as a youth movement counselor in Giv'atayim, a suburb of Tel Aviv. My task, and that of five other counselors with whom I shared a three-bedroom apartment, was to inculcate kibbutz values and shepherd the teenagers' development into a cohesive group that would enter the Nahal division of the IDF together. After completing their service, they were to fulfill the youth movement's ideals and join a kibbutz. I was supposed to be both a role model and a practical guide on how to be a perfect kibbutznik. My IDF tour of duty would be in the service of the greater goal of leading idealistic city youth to the utopia of the kibbutz. I was "all in"—serving in the army would be a natural continuation of my year as a youth movement counselor, and I hoped to have ample opportunities to support, encourage, and inspire my charges.

I had it all mapped out. After six weeks of basic training, three months of the NCO course, and another six weeks of supervising recruits, I would move on to a Nahal post organized like a small kibbutz, where I would be able to follow my calling. And, in addition to my duties as an advisor, counselor, inspiration, and guide, the actual military machinations—marching, drills, saluting, and roll call—would be minimal. I had had my fill of those by the second week of basic training.

Right after that live-fire drill, the base commander summoned me to her office. I suppose I had demonstrated courage and equanimity under fire and, thus, had shown I was "officer material." I entered the office and saluted.

"Congratulations," the commander beamed at me. She stretched out her hand to shake mine. "You made the grade. You are going to officer's training."

"But . . ." I stammered.

I had prepared a meticulously structured explanation for why I didn't want to be an officer. I had known in advance that I was likely to be selected. I had been honored as an "Outstanding Soldier" in both basic training and the NCO course. What could I do? Like it or not, I seemed to make a good soldier.

My argument against becoming an officer was threefold. First, while Israel was, for the most part, still in the euphoric post–Six-Day-War state of mind, I was becoming more politically aware, critical, and opposed to the Occupation. I did not want to actively aid in the army's job of maintaining the Occupation of the West Bank and supporting the new settlements that dotted the Jordan Valley, Gush Etzion (an enclave near Hebron), the Sinai, and the Golan Heights. (Later, in the late '70s, after Menachem Begin's ascension to power, they proliferated in the heartland of the West Bank.) I was hoping to be stationed at a Nahal settlement in an area that had, as its only *raison d'etre*, being a border security outpost, and where there were no prospects of its turning into a civilian community.

Second, I was deeply influenced by my epistolary boyfriend, David, and his opposition to the Vietnam War. At his suggestion, I was reading *Catch 22* (Joseph Heller's 1961 satirical novel about serving in the American military), which made it hard to be enthusiastic about any military system or bureaucracy. My third reason was that, as an officer, I would spend most of my army service supervising one cohort after another of female recruits, a rather rote process highlighting army discipline and marching in military formation, of little value to the actual operations of the army. Instead, I wanted to serve where I could develop real relationships with the female soldiers under my command. My past year as a youth movement counselor had influenced me deeply and, perhaps, my yet-unknown future as a social worker was already in the making.

By the time of this summons to the commander's office I had already taken my first gingerly step towards irreverence in the face of the army's strict regimens. I was growing a big Afro. The army

Upper left, I had a "pre-Afro" on Conscription Day. *Upper right,* I had a full Afro on graduating from non-commissioned officer training. *Left,* my self-portrait.

required female soldiers to keep their hair either short, in a bun, or in a pinned-up braid so it didn't touch their collar. My hairstyle presented my commanders with an irritating dilemma. The Afro met the length regulations: my hair never brushed my neckband. But the width and height of my hairdo certainly did not conform to military

David Biale and I in the spring of 1972.

style. It couldn't be outlawed because it violated no rules. Against their wishes, the commanders had to allow it.

I had won the hair battle for now but, surely, being an officer would entail much stricter adherence to military form and function. The Afro would have to go.

"But . . ." I repeated looking my commander straight in the eye, "I don't want to be an officer."

She frowned momentarily but didn't even bother to ask for my reasons.

"What you want is of no interest to the IDF. You are ordered to take the exam."

"But . . ."

"At ease. Excused!"

So I took the earliest bus from the base to Tel Aviv, to the IDF administrative headquarters. I wound my way through meandering paths between ramshackle barracks and dilapidated offices, looking for the hall where the exam was held. Getting lost seemed like an attractive possibility and an elegant way out, but too many soldiers stationed at the base came to my aid and showed me the way.

I knew I couldn't cheat by giving purposefully wrong answers on the aptitude test. The army already had my records from the induction process, and there, I knew, my scores were rather high. I dutifully completed the test, seeing no way to escape. But then, eureka! The very last page was a declaration sheet: "Sign here _____ indicating your agreement to serve in the army an extra six months upon passing the test and completing the Officer's Training Course."

I walked up to the test monitor, a major, old enough to be doing this as his reserve duty service.

"I have a problem," I said.

He motioned me to come to the side of his small desk and keep my voice low, so as not to disturb other candidates still laboring at the toughest questions.

"This, here," I pointed to the declaration, "implies that I am willingly agreeing to go to the officers' course, and I am not."

"You are not what?" he frowned.

"Willingly going to the officers' course."

He looked at me, at the paper, and then examined my face more closely. I tried for an innocent, yet determined, expression.

"You don't want to go to officers' training. That's what you mean?"

"Exactly," I nodded.

"Then what are you doing here?"

"I was ordered to come."

He thought about it for a minute. Getting into officers' training was generally both sought after and very competitive. He took my papers, both the declaration and the completed test, and said, "So, go home!"

"So I'm out? My test will not be scored?" I asked.

"Not on my watch!" he barked.

I went back to my base and reported to my commander. She pursed her lips in frustration. She couldn't charge me with insubordination; I had followed protocol to a T, and the test monitor's rank was much higher than hers. The next day, I found myself assigned to be a basic training NCO for another cohort. As far as I was concerned, I was consigned to putting my life on the line again for a few weeks just so female soldiers would know how to shoot a gun that they would never use after basic training.

But I got lucky. Perhaps an officer on the base who was from my kibbutz, a year older than me but a childhood friend, had intervened on my behalf. Or maybe the top commander decided that between my Afro and my attitude, I was not a good role model. Either way, after the second rotation commanding fresh recruits, I was ordered to report for a new deployment and stationed at Mitzpeh Shalem, just as I had hoped.

It was situated in a desolate, Godforsaken spot overlooking the Dead Sea. A dirt road branched off from the paved one, hugging the banks. Barely wide enough to accommodate cars, the dirt road climbed through a moonscape of canyons and rock outcroppings, winding in switchbacks up the nearly one thousand feet of elevation to the edge of the Judean desert plateau. One bus arrived daily at 4:00 p.m. from Jerusalem, turned around, and headed right back. If you got there at any other time, by hitchhiking or being dropped off by a different bus (which went further south to Ein Gedi), you would call up to the office on a field phone nailed to a wooden post at the intersection. All you could do was beg for someone to come fetch you. If no one could, you hiked up.

At Mitzpeh Shalem, my colleague and I were the two NCOs in charge of the female soldiers. We held roll call every afternoon, but in truth we mostly functioned as advisors and counselors to the young women. I had girls who came from abusive families and were afraid to go home for weekends. Others needed emotional support because they had never been away from home and were terribly homesick. And, of course, many had boyfriend problems.

To my great relief I found out at the first roll call that the female soldiers were issued old-fashioned Czech-made rifles (used in Israel's 1948 War of Independence) but no bullets. The main purpose of the weapons was, it seemed, instilling the discipline of daily cleaning. Never again would I have to stand behind newly minted soldiers with live fire in their hands. It was no longer dangerous to turn around and look back. "At ease!" I said to myself with a sigh of relief. Now that I could look back, I could also look forward: after the army . . . where was my life heading?

CHAPTER 25

Desert Treasures

"Who is that?" I whispered to my partner NCO at Mitzpeh Shalem. We were at the dining room table, my first breakfast at Mitzpeh Shalem. I nodded towards an old man lining up with the soldiers and loading his tray with vegetables, yogurt, and eggs. He looked to be eighty years old, with Ben Gurion-like shocks of wild white hair at his temples. (In fact, he was born in 1907, so at the time he was sixty-five). He was wearing rumpled work clothes, like those the men on my kibbutz wore during my childhood in the 1950s. He held a pipe in his left hand and carried the tray of food in his right. On the edge of his tray lay a rusty trowel.

"That's Pesach," she whispered back. "I'll tell you later."

After breakfast she explained that Pesach Bar Adon, the famous archeologist, was living with us on the base as a permanent guest so he could pursue his excavations in the surrounding hills. He mostly found remains of prehistoric habitation: stone circles marked spots where homes had been, and stone tools verified the presence of humans. Pesach rejoiced with every fist-held hammer, serrated blade, or arrowhead. But what he was really looking for, I realized after I read up on him, was a second "Cave of the Treasure." He had uncovered one in 1961 in Nahal Mishmar, only twenty kilometers south of us. It stood to reason there would be more.

That treasure trove he found in 1961 included over four hundred stunningly beautiful copper artifacts, along with a few pieces carved from hippopotamus ivory and one from an elephant's tusk. They dated back to at least 3,500 BCE. Most of the objects seemed to have no practical use. Displayed in the Israel Museum in Jerusalem, their captions read: "For unknown ritual purpose."

Nothing like it had been found by anyone else. Pesach had been looking for over a decade, a lone man scouring the desert for treasures. He was delighted to hear that I was interested in archeology. I mentioned that my mother had worked with Yigael Yadin at Masada. A cloud passed over his eyes. "Eh . . . crazy mass suicide . . ." he let slip, referring to the nearly one thousand men, women, and children who committed mass suicide rather than be captured by the Roman soldiers who breached the walls of the fortified outpost in the Judean desert. Pesach never got the kind of publicity and admiration lavished on Yadin and Masada. Perhaps this was so because the mysterious objects he found testified to a highly sophisticated material culture of a lost civilization that predated the Hebrews by millennia, and was therefore of no use for the national narrative of heroism.

Pesach was taken aback when I asked what I needed to do to qualify to work with him. "Just come," he smiled. "I start at dawn; the early light is excellent for discerning unusual contours in the earth."

"What do you mean by 'unusual contours?'" I was already hooked.

"Stone semicircles or square corners. They indicate man-made structures."

"That's what you're looking for?"

"Yes, human habitation. And stone tools."

"Not scrolls?" I asked naïvely. Mitzpeh Shalem was less than twenty-five kilometers south of the Qumran Caves, where the Dead Sea Scrolls had been found.

"Eh . . ." Pesach muttered, "recent history. We're looking for remains of the Chalcolithic Period, at least three thousand years earlier. *That* is archeology."

So, my work assignment was digging with Pesach. No one had done that before; it was not a vital function. The settlement was organized like a small kibbutz, so in addition to fairly minimal military functions (guard posts along the perimeter fence and a morning sweep outside it), all the soldiers and commanders worked in typical kibbutz jobs, growing vegetables and melons in the fields down by the Dead Sea shores, and carrying out kitchen, laundry, and office tasks. Since I was a commander, I pulled rank: "Digging with Pesach" was added to the *siddur avodah,* the daily work allotment schedule, and soon others asked for a chance to do it.

Commanding some twenty female soldiers, my co-commander and I held roll call every afternoon. We checked the girls' rooms for cleanliness and order. Blankets had to be folded and stacked at the bottom of the bed just so. We checked the windowsills for dust. We sniffed the bathrooms to make sure Lysol fumes were in the air. The military function was inspecting their rifles for sand in the barrel, unavoidable in such a dusty place. Other than sand traps, those rifles really had no function. They were old Czech-produced guns, which had been essential for Israel's survival in the War of Independence in 1948. Now they were used for training, military parades, and arming female soldiers. In basic training we were each issued such a rifle and slept with it under our mattress. On night guard duty at the outskirts of the large camp, we were issued two bullets in a plastic bag. We joked that, should we suspect an intruder, our orders were to call out, "Halt! Halt or I'll open the plastic bag!"

Pesach passed by during roll call one afternoon and waved hello.

"Come over," I called him, "and tell these girls what you used this rifle for in your day."

"What for?" he asked with a puzzled frown.

"They need to understand the history," I said, "that we are not issuing them these guns just to make their lives miserable cleaning out the endless sand."

The girls sat down in a circle, their rifles in their laps, and listened to Pesach. At first they seemed uninterested and distracted, lavishing most of their attention on their lacquered nails. But gradually Pesach enchanted them. He was a master storyteller who'd got his start writing children's books about his life with Bedouin shepherds in the early 1930s. He'd spent several years in Transjordan and Mandatory Palestine under the *nom de guerre* Aziz Effendi, in order to gain insight into the biblical lives of the nomadic shepherds of ancient Israel. The Bedouin had maintained that way of life into the twentieth century.

He spoke of his days in the Haganah, before the State of Israel was established. He'd been stationed in the Yemin Moshe neighborhood in Jerusalem in 1936–39, protecting the inhabitants during the Arab Revolt (against the British Mandatory Authorities and Jewish immigration). Later he participated in clandestine operations, smuggling immigrants who lacked British-issued entry certificates into Palestine. He also participated in running contraband arms for the War of Independence. "In fact," he exclaimed, "I smuggled in these very Czech rifles you now sneer at." The soldiers hung on his every word, dumbfounded as pages from the history book they had memorized for their matriculation exams came alive in front of their very eyes.

In those turbulent times before 1948, Pesach had often carried a "Czechi" rifle or a pistol. But nowadays, he roamed the hills around Mitzpeh Shalem unarmed, feeling completely safe. The occasional Bedouin he ran into usually recognized him; that man, his father, or his uncle had dug with Pesach at the Cave of the Treasure.

We all felt very safe in Mitzpeh Shalem and considered the strict procedures for guarding the place unnecessary, just one of those things an army would insist on. But one Sunday an urgent warning of potential intruders burst our secure bubble. At dawn, I was roused, along with David, my boyfriend, who had spent the weekend with me, by a siren and loudspeaker announcement. All the female soldiers were ordered to run into the bomb shelter, with their rifles, but still no bullets. The male soldiers grabbed their guns—real ones, M16s and Uzis—and deployed around the perimeter. Around 8:00 a.m. the "All clear" was announced. No intruders had been found. A small section of the perimeter fence had been trampled, possibly by an infiltrator. But a stray goat or donkey could equally have been the culprit.

We all streamed to the dining room for a cold breakfast, as no cooking had been done that morning. Pesach ambled into the dining room, his clothes already dusty and the trowel in his hand.

"Where have you been?" barked the commanding officer.

"Out digging, what else?"

"Didn't you here the alarm at 5:00 a.m.? You were under orders to go to the shelter?"

"What for?"

"There were infiltrators nearby, possibly terrorists attempting to set bombs."

"Eh," Pesach shrugged dismissively, "if there were any so-called infiltrators they would have been just local Bedouin trying to steal stuff. I know all of them."

"What are you talking about?" The commander was still fuming.

"I know them," Pesach repeated. "They used to dig with me before this place was put up. I still see them around and talk to them."

"You talk to them? How?"

"Of course. I'm fluent in Arabic. Back in the thirties I used to live with the Bedouin."

What could the commander say about a time long before he'd been born?

I went digging with Pesach every week. I never discovered any significant archeological artifacts, but I found a fascinating man and a wonderful friendship. He was the personification of the Israel that no longer existed: pioneering, humble, idealistic, and modest to the point of poverty. David and I once visited him in his apartment on Palmach Street in Jerusalem. He made us dinner of sardines and eggs, fried on a *ptiliya*—a field stove that had been army issue in the

Archeologist Pesach
Bar Adon during
the "Cave of the
Treasure"
excavations.
Courtesy of his son,
Doron Bar Adon.

1948 war. He'd probably kept it since then, as he had the mess kit tin plates he used for serving the meal. Other than a postage stamp-sized kitchen, a very narrow bed (I suspected an army cot also issued to him in 1948), and some shelves nearly collapsing under the weight of books, the whole apartment was floor to ceiling piles of cigarette cartons and shoeboxes.

Those boxes turned out to be Pesach's storage system for the artifacts he excavated. A chain smoker, he always had a cigarette box in his shirt pockets when digging. As the cigarettes went out, the flint tool shards went in. If he found something larger, he stowed it in a leather pouch tied to the rope that served as his belt. At the end of the day, the cigarettes were all gone and the cigarette box was nearly bursting with the day's finds. After work, the pipe came out, indicating leisure time.

I was drawn to a black-and-white photograph in a simple frame, lodged between stacks of boxes. I leaned close to it: Pesach, a bit younger but still with those wings of white hair, seated in an IDF jeep next to an IDF officer in the driver's seat. The World War II-era goggles I had seen in a photo of Pesach (from the 1961 excavation of the Cave of the Treasure) were hanging from his neck.

"What's this photo?" I asked

It was taken on June 8, 1967, Pesach said. The story rolled out, as if a ribbon had fallen down, unspooling as it rolled along the floor.

Stranded at home for the third day because of the Six-Day War, his phone had rung.

"We're on our way to take Hebron," his son, an IDF lieutenant in the paratroopers, shouted over his field telephone. "Want to come along?"

"Sure," Pesach said.

"Get ready. I'll be at your place in my jeep in ten minutes. Take your goggles; it might be very dusty."

"I'm ready already," replied Pesach, who wore the same work clothes every day, whether digging in the desert or at home in Jerusalem. He reached for a new packet of cigarettes, the goggles, and his trowel . . . just in case an opportunity arose.

The jeep arrived shortly and Pesach hopped in. They raced on dirt roads to join his son's unit at the outskirts of Hebron. The soldiers were assembled in a big semicircle to hear Shlomo Goren, the chief rabbi of the IDF. He had demanded to address them before the attack began, "to inspire them and strengthen their resolve." He was a general, so the commanding officer had no choice but to offer him the wooden crate podium.

Goren stepped up. In one hand he held a shofar and in the other an open Bible. "Deuteronomy, chapter 20," he announced and began to read in a booming voice:

> When you go to war against your enemies and see horses and chariots and an army greater than yours, do not be afraid of them, because the LORD your God, who brought you up out of Egypt, will be with you. . . .
>
> In the cities of the nations the LORD your God is giving you as an inheritance, do not leave alive anything that breathes."

"*Lo techayeh kol neshamah!*" he bellowed the last sentence again. Then he blew the shofar three times.

"Not for me . . ." Pesach whispered to his son.

"Not for me, either," his son said softly.

As he told the story, Pesach was visibly agitated. He shook his head and muttered, "It's not my country anymore."

"I am old," he said after a moment of silence, "but you two are young. You'll change it, bring it back to what it was."

I didn't say anything, but I didn't think we could.

CHAPTER 26

Turning Forward, Turning Back

"So, where shall we go?" David and I kept circling back to the same question. We had already decided we would study in the United States the next year, David for a PhD and I for a BA. But where?

Ever since I had come back from the high school year in America, I had a notion that I wanted to go back there for college. I had no plan or strategy for making it happen, and it only dawned on me very slowly, as the relationship with David deepened and imagining our lives entwined seemed more real, that this is how it would come about: we would study in the US together. I took the SAT and TOEFL (Test of English as a Foreign Language) exams at the US Cultural Center on Keren Ha-Yesod Street in Jerusalem. It was a purposefully modest place, serving to clarify that the United States Embassy would remain in Tel Aviv until the status of Jerusalem was determined in a peace treaty.[16]

When my reasonably good scores came back, my imaginings

---

16. It would remain in Tel Aviv for decades until the arrival of Trump.

began to take shape as a potential reality. The idea of marriage and a wedding came later. It was the seventies: who thought of such bourgeois niceties? But it was precisely the anti-bourgeois, purist egalitarianism of the kibbutz that forced the issue.

"You realize," my mother said one day at the beginning of December, "that if you and David decide to get married when you're in the US, the kibbutz may not approve our request for a trip to the wedding." I hadn't thought of it but, indeed, that seemed fairly likely. The kibbutz did permit members to go abroad at the community's expense for special family situations, but a wedding all the way in California might be beyond its financial means. In addition, since my parents had already been to the US in 1967, they were the last ones in the queue for a trip abroad.

Early on the morning of December 10, 1972, exactly thirty-three years from the day my mother left her hometown, David and I set down the first stepping-stone in my long journey away from my birthplace. We were talking in bed at David's student apartment in Jerusalem.

"So . . . my mother said," I started and relayed the conversation from a week or so before.

"Hmm . . ." he said.

I explained her reasoning.

"Well, then, I guess we'll get married here," David replied, "before we go. Why not?"

That was the extent of "The Proposal," and we woke up one of David's closest Berkeley friends who happened to be visiting us, and made our announcement. He toasted us with the only non-H_2O liquid in the house: a glass of orange juice.

We planned our kibbutz wedding for March 20, 1973, the first day of spring. We got married on the kibbutz in an unusual blend of the kibbutz-style wedding and an observant one. Most kibbutz weddings involved a *chuppah* (refers to both the canopy and a Jewish wedding ceremony) outdoors, with the rabbinate-sent rabbi from nearby Beit She'an. He would read the *ketubah* (marriage contract) and recite the

My wedding. Rabbi Chaim Druckman shakes hands
with David.

marriage formula and the seven blessings at breakneck speed. No
one paid much attention until the final breaking of the glass and
thundering "Mazal tov!" by the members standing around in a big
circle. Now the kibbutz spirit took over, and a procession with singing headed inside the dining room where a festive meal was followed
by the highlight: skits and songs about the newlyweds performed by
the best musical talents of the community and toasts by the couples'
friends and kibbutz leaders and co-workers.

David and I were deeply immersed in charting our path to a
deeper relationship to Jewish tradition so we did things very differ-
ently. We asked Rabbi Chaim Druckman (with whom I had studied
in the monthly "Judaism seminar" I attended since high school) to
officiate and conduct the chuppah in a deliberate manner, explaining
the meaning and customs of each step. We went as far as holding the
chuppah indoors, in the kibbutz's auditorium—a break from tradition—in order to make sure people really paid attention. Indeed, the
kibbutz members were intrigued, and many told me afterwards
they'd never realized "there's so much in this ceremony."

When we got to the breaking of the glass at the end, it turned out we'd forgotten to bring a wine glass to be stepped on. One of our chuppah pole holders chugged down the nearly full glass of wine (thick and overly sweet, similar to Manischewitz) and handed the empty glass to David to break. It was Duralex tempered glass, so breaking it with his foot was not easy. But David managed and was rewarded with an uproarious "Mazal tov." Then everyone marched halfway across the kibbutz to the old dining room for dancing. Then a busload of our guests, who had been stranded on the Jerusalem-Jericho road by a mechanical problem, burst in, singing and clapping.

The usual kibbutz celebration of songs and skits composed especially for the newlyweds was set aside because shortly before our wedding the community was shocked by the untimely death of a very prominent member. No one was in the mood to write songs and skits, and we agreed with the culture coordinator's suggestion of bringing a popular "pre-packaged" program from the Kibbutz Movement Culture Department in Tel Aviv: a multimedia presentation of slides accompanied by a soundtrack of music and readings. The theme: "The Song of Songs." That seemed very appropriate, combining the themes of love and spring.

Rabbi Druckman, who had performed the chuppah so beautifully, was seated near our family. A deeply religious Orthodox Jewish man, he was, at the time, very involved in bridging the gap between the religious and secular camps of Israeli society. He had brought his near-bar-mitzvah-aged son with him, probably to show him a beautiful example of this bridging effort. After the meal everyone turned towards the screen at the front of the room, and the presentation began to roll. It opened with gorgeous flute music, a sonorous recitation of verses from *Shir Ha-Shirim*, the Song of Songs, and images of ripening wheat fields and budding apple trees. I relaxed into my chair, thinking, *This will be lovely.*

But soon the slides began to shift and now we had pictures of a naked young man and nubile woman running through those fields as the narrator read: "Listen! My beloved! Look, here he comes, leaping across the mountains; bounding over the hills" and "Come my beloved let us go to the field . . . let us go to the vineyards to see if the vines have budded, their blossoms opened, the pomegranates in bloom." My face drained of blood, and I turned to look at Rabbi Druckman. He sat stoically erect, as did his son. Their eyes were cast down, glued to the bright white tablecloth, or perhaps the crumbs now strewn on it. But you wouldn't have known anything was amiss if you didn't look closely. He never said anything, other than that he had a three-hour drive home, when he took his leave soon after the program ended.

In early 1974, he became well known in Israel as one of the leaders of the extreme right-wing settler movement, Gush Emunim. To my chagrin, I was told that everyone on my kibbutz said, "That's Racheli's rabbi!" I prayed (so to speak) that it wasn't those naked—to him pornographic—pictures that pushed him over the edge to the far right.

Marrying in March meant I was able to get out of the army a few months ahead of my anticipated release time. That would allow us to travel in Europe for a month on a honeymoon and work at a Zionist Youth Movement summer camp in upstate New York, before heading to UCLA to start our studies at the beginning of September. On the other hand, getting married torpedoed our original plan to study at Brandeis, where I was awarded a very handsome fellowship for foreign students. When the university authorities found out that by the time I arrived there I would be a married woman, they withdrew the offer. The fellowship was meant to promote foreign students mingling with the American ones in the dorms. There were no dorms for married students, and surely a married woman would be much less interested in the desired mingling. So we deployed "Plan B" and were heading to UCLA and David's hometown of Los Angeles.

Had I returned to the kibbutz after completing my army service, I would have been eligible to become a member and the kibbutz would have provided me with a ten- by twelve-foot room of my own (shared bathroom outside), an iron twin-sized bed frame (like the one David, Navah, and I hid under during the shelling in the summer of 1970) with mattress and bedding, a one-drawer night stand, and two chairs. I took the cash instead: sixty liras, enough to buy those items second-hand. Leaving the kibbutz was seen in those days as an act of betrayal, so you certainly couldn't expect to get rich on it.

A few weeks after the wedding, I got my final army release and US visa. We packed my few possessions and got a ride with a kibbutz member driving to Tel Aviv to set off on a honeymoon trip in Europe and then to America! My mother accompanied us. At the North Tel Aviv train station, we said good-bye and boarded the shuttle bus to the airport. My mother continued to town, planning to spend the night with friends and return to the kibbutz the next day. Years later she told me she spent three hours walking the streets in Tel Aviv in a daze, trying to hold back her tears, while I blithely boarded the bus, not turning around, not looking back, not comprehending what part-ing at a train station meant to her.

Over four decades passed before I read the English translation of my mother's diary entry of December 10, 1939, describing leaving her family at the Masaryk train station in Prague.

Finally I understood.

EPILOGUE

David and I came back to Israel time and again, first as students and then as young professionals, including once for a year. Later we came with our children. Several of these visits were opportunities to examine if and how we could go back permanently. But none of the potential situations, first at Kibbutz Gezer with friends, then Jerusalem, later Haifa University, were a good fit. Eventually we realized we never would. It took two decades for me to make my peace with this, and even longer for my family to accept and forgive my leaving the kibbutz and Israel. My parents and two brothers with their families anchored us in Kfar Ruppin. I, however, continued the chain of migration, which began with my grandparents departing their families' rural hearths for Prague, and my parents' leaving their beloved hometown.

Five decades after they had left Prague, following the 1989 "Velvet Revolution" that peacefully brought down Communist rule in Czechoslovakia, my parents returned, together with my siblings and me, traveling "back home." My brothers were enchanted, seeing the city's beauty for the first time. I had already been there under Communism, during grim, gray days. Now the aura of liberation, along with restorations and renovations, gave everything a new glow.

"What I can't understand," my brother Eran said as he swept his open palm across Prague's gleaming Old Town Square, "is how you went from here . . . to there," meaning our humble kibbutz at the end of an isolated, narrow road.

Of course, there is a simple answer: youthful idealism coinciding with the crushing boot of history. Kfar Ruppin was, indeed, a far cry from Prague. Summers were intolerably hot and stiflingly dusty.

They had no fans. Winters were frigid. The dust turned to thick mud that sucked your boots into its hungry maw; you had to wrest them out with both hands. My mother got bronchitis every winter, and asthma and heat rashes each summer. Culture was homemade for the first twenty years; the cafés, museums, and concert halls of their youth in Prague only wistful memories. But my parents lived at the kibbutz for the rest of their lives, even as they watched how their utopian dreams all too often gave way to pettiness and power struggles.

Their "Great Expectations" were not exactly dashed but, rather, like all dreams, they gradually gave way to realism and compromise. Yet their dreams did create a thrilling, carefree, and empowering childhood for us on the kibbutz. I now look back at it with wonder. I cherish the heady freedom, the independence, and the deep sense of mutual responsibility embedded in my psyche. I marvel at how we romped through the kibbutz and the hills and fields surrounding it, feeling like we owned the place. I remember proudly how we changed Sammi's wet sheet at 5:00 a.m. and how we stood vigil over Arik the night he banged his head on the doorpost. I cherish how excited I was at my own courage when I walked through the fields alone in the dark to our "camp" near the Jordan river, though I also remember how scared I was. At the same time, I am astonished that our parents gave us this intoxicating freedom and autonomy, and blithely went about their business, certain that we not only would not be killed or maimed, but in fact would flourish and become strong.

My classmates dispersed after graduating from high school and serving in the army. Three of us went far, to live in the United States, Canada, and New Zealand. The rest mostly scattered in various communities in Israel. Four of them died: Rafi in the Yom Kippur War, Amos (my first cousin) in the crash of an ultralight plane he was piloting, and two others from cancer.

Only two remain at the kibbutz. One is Arik, who has benefited in the kibbutz's close-knit supportive community, which created optimal conditions for someone with intellectual limitations to live a full life. The other is Dorit, who married a man from the neighboring kibbutz, and lives in a one-street neighborhood of the kibbutz for non-member residents. They live a kind of à la carte kibbutz life, picking and choosing the aspects from which they wish to benefit and those to which they wish to contribute. I live so very far away. This book is what I chose to contribute: to the kibbutz that was, and to whatever it may become.

ACKNOWLEDGMENTS

I want to thank friends and colleagues who have read or listened to some of the stories included in this book. They provided enthusiastic support and helpful pointers about what worked and what needed more work. They include Sara Bolder, Diane Wolf, Sam Norich, Debbie Ugoretz, Fania Oz-Salzberger, Carol Cosman, Robert Alter, Chana Kronfeld, Noam Zion, Yudit Rosenberg, and Assaf Inbari. I read and discussed portions of the work with Naomi Seidman and Marcia Friedman at our periodic writing group meetings. Their helpful comments were always right on the mark, offered in friendship and support.

Bonny V. Fetterman served as my keen-eyed editor, agent, and enthusiastic supporter throughout the whole process. Her insight and wisdom enhanced the work and buoyed my spirits through the trying process of finding a publisher. It was a special treat to reconnect and work together after thirty-five years had passed since she edited my *Women and Jewish Law* at Schocken Books. We've forged a wonderful collaboration and friendship. Dr. Robert Mandel, at Mandel Vilar Press, was enthusiastic and gracious from our first contact and has supported the process with consummate judgment and care. My thanks also to the rest of the Mandel Vilar team: Mary Beth Hinton, who copyedited the work with a precision and care that is a rarity in publishing today; Barbara Werden, who provided the same careful attention to the photographs; and Sophie Appel, who designed the beautiful cover.

My family in Kfar Ruppin and throughout Israel has not yet read this book (except for Oded who read early versions of some of the stories): they (and I) are hoping and waiting for the Hebrew translation. My grown kids, Noam and Tali, read early versions and provided incisive comments about style and storylines, as well as pointing out lacunae, such as things about kibbutz life that a general reader would not understand. They have their own vivid memories of visits to Kfar Ruppin and the Korati family, and it was enlightening to see my kibbutz and, in some ways, myself through their eyes.

My husband, David, started this journey with me by hiding together under the bed during a shelling at my kibbutz on a summer evening in 1970. Everything in my life since then has flowed and flowered from that night. He has been my beloved, my partner, my editor, and my support.

ABOUT THE AUTHOR

Rachel Biale was born in 1952 and raised on Kibbutz Kfar Ruppin, by the Jordan River. After serving in the Israel Defense Forces, she came to the United States in 1973, earning her bachelor of arts and master of arts degrees in Jewish history from the University of California Los Angeles and a master's degree in social work from the Wurzweiler School of Social Work at Yeshiva University. Rachel is a clinical social worker. She has worked as a therapist specializing in families and young children, and has had a parenting counseling practice for over thirty years. She has also worked as an adult Jewish education program director, a teacher, and a community organizer.

Her first book, *Women and Jewish Law* (Schocken, 1984), is considered a groundbreaking book in Jewish studies and remains in print. She also authored and illustrated three children's books, one in Hebrew and two in English: *The Old Clock* (1975), *We Are Moving: A Let's Make a Book about It Book* (1996), and *My Pet Died: A Let's Make a Book about It Book* (1997). Rachel also wrote a parenting advice column for the San Francisco Bay Area Jewish community newspaper. Her parenting advice book, *What Now? 2-Minute Tips for Solving Common Parenting Challenges*, will be published in April 2020. She also writes and illuminates Jewish marriage contracts (*ketubot*).

Rachel is a seasoned public speaker. She has taught university courses and presented lectures at community centers, adult education programs, and Jewish cultural institutions in the US, Israel, and Europe. She resides with her husband in Berkeley.